A DEAL WITH THE DEVIL

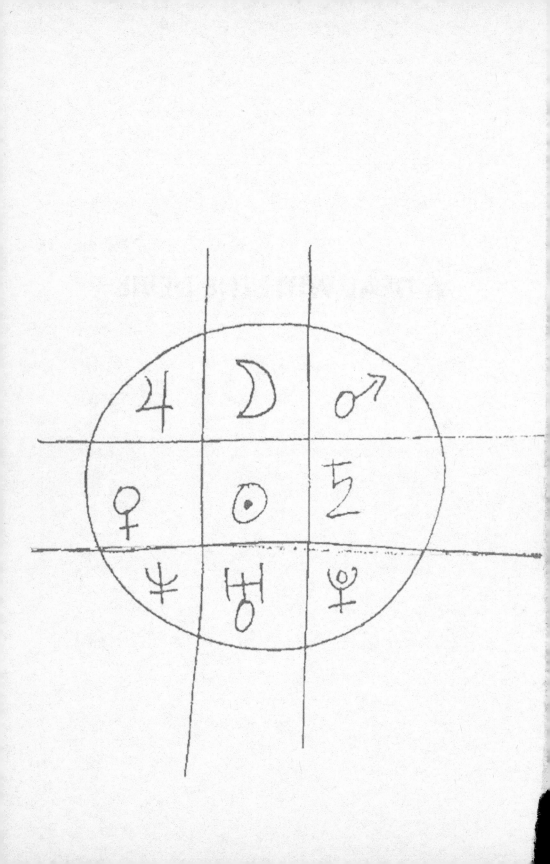

A DEAL WITH THE DEVIL

The Dark and Twisted True Story of One of the Biggest Cons in History

BLAKE ELLIS and **MELANIE HICKEN**

ATRIA BOOKS

New York • London • Toronto • Sydney • New Delhi

ATRIA
BOOKS

An Imprint of Simon & Schuster, Inc.
1230 Avenue of the Americas
New York, NY 10020

First Atria Books hardcover edition August 2018

ATRIA BOOKS and colophon are trademarks of Simon & Schuster, Inc.

For information about special discounts for bulk purchases, please contact Simon & Schuster Special Sales at 1-866-506-1949 or business@simonandschuster.com.

The Simon & Schuster Speakers Bureau can bring authors to your live event. For more information or to book an event, contact the Simon & Schuster Speakers Bureau at 1-866-248-3049 or visit our website at www.simonspeakers.com.

Interior design by Dana Sloan

Manufactured in the United States of America

10 9 8 7 6 5 4 3 2 1

Library of Congress Cataloging-in-Publication Data

Names: Ellis, Blake, author. | Hicken, Melanie, author.
Title: A deal with the devil : the dark and twisted true story of one of the
  biggest cons in history / Blake Ellis, Melanie Hicken.
Description: New York : Atria Books, 2018. | Includes bibliographical references.
Identifiers: LCCN 2017055494 (print) | LCCN 2018013379 (ebook) | ISBN
  9781501163869 (Ebook) | ISBN 9781501163845 (hardback) | ISBN 9781501163852
  (paperback)
Subjects: LCSH: Swindlers and swindling. | Victims of crimes—Psychology. |
  Crime—History—21st century. | BISAC: TRUE CRIME / General.
Classification: LCC HV6691 (ebook) | LCC HV6691 .E445 2018 (print) | DDC
  364.16/3—dc23
LC record available at https://lccn.loc.gov/2017055494

ISBN 978-1-5011-6384-5
ISBN 978-1-5011-6386-9 (ebook)

For Lex Haris, who let two reporters spend months

chasing down a French psychic

The first thing I noticed when I met Maria Duval were her eyes. Cat's eyes. Not the blue eyes of a Siamese cat, with the shade of delft-blue porcelain china. Not the eyes of a Persian cat, with the shade of molten gold. The eyes of a street cat. Mysterious green, with the sea-blue shades of a swamp. Lights with the sparkle of golden coins, glowworms, and star particles. We stood opposite each other. Maria looked straight into my eyes. People say that a cheetah hypnotizes its prey before he strikes. That is what I had in front of me. A cheetah. A captivating catlike woman who held me in the grip of her emerald-green eyes.

—UNKNOWN

Contents

PART 3

PART 4

Cast of Characters

Alain: An archivist at the French newspaper *Nice-Matin*

Astroforce: A company long connected to the Maria Duval letters that was used on business filings around the world and of which Maria Duval was once a shareholder

Françoise Barre: Former mayor of Callas and close friend of Maria Duval

Willem Bosma: A Dutch journalist who spoke with Jacques Mailland when reporting on the Maria Duval scam in the Netherlands

Anne Chamfort: Another purported French psychic whose face and name have been used for letters very similar to Maria's

Data Marketing Group Ltd.: A Long Island–based company that tracked payments from victims and fulfilled orders for talismans

Destiny Research Center: An apparent shell company used to mask where the most recent US Maria Duval letters were coming from

Joseph Patrick Davitt: An Australian businessman listed as director of Listano Limited, the owner of Maria Duval trademarks

Martin Dettling: The mysterious Swiss man who opened the mailboxes in Sparks, Nevada

Maria Duval: A purported French psychic whose name, image, and signature have appeared on millions of psychic letters sent around the world

Andrea Egger: The Swiss attorney who helped file a number of Maria Duval trademarks around the world and whom we attempted to confront in Monaco

gd2use: Online handle of a mysterious person who uploaded numerous videos of Maria Duval interviews to YouTube

Clayton Gerber: The US postal inspector whom we first interviewed about the Maria Duval scam, who said it was one of the largest consumer frauds in history

Patrick Guerin: Maria Duval's psychic sidekick, who appears in some of her letters and advertises in-person consultations in Paris

Infogest: A Swiss company founded by Jean-Claude Reuille that once managed the worldwide distribution of the Maria Duval letters

Infogest Direct Marketing: A Canadian company connected to the Swiss Infogest, which managed the mailing of the Maria Duval letters in the United States and Canada

Julia Jones: A French-speaking CNN reporter

Jacques Mailland: A French copywriter and alleged mastermind of the Maria Duval letters

Jordan Malter: A CNN producer who filmed our journey

Lukas Mattle: A former Infogest employee

Barney McGettigan: A British accountant in Stratford-upon-Avon whose firm provided the mailing address for Listano Limited

Thomas Ninan: A US postal inspector and key investigator for the US government's Maria Duval case

PacNet Services: A Canadian payment processor that cashed many of the checks mailed to the Maria Duval scam over the years

Antoine Palfroy: The son of Maria Duval and former owner of an eccentric bookshop

Gerard du Passage: A man now living in Thailand who had previously served as a contact for Maria Duval

Patric: A man claiming to be Jean-Claude Reuille's childhood friend who contacted us after our Maria Duval series ran

Luis Alberto Ramos: A man who sued Maria Duval after she purchased a field from him in Argentina but allegedly never paid for it

Jean-Claude Reuille: A Swiss businessman and alleged ringleader of the Maria Duval letters

Chrissie Robinson: A woman who tried for years to save her mother, Doreen, from the grip of the Maria Duval scam

Doreen Robinson: An elderly woman and mother of Chrissie, who became obsessed with Maria Duval while battling dementia

Jan Vanlangendonck: A Belgian journalist who interviewed Maria Duval in a Parisian café

Véronique: A psychic in Callas who was the first person we found who actually claimed to have met Maria Duval

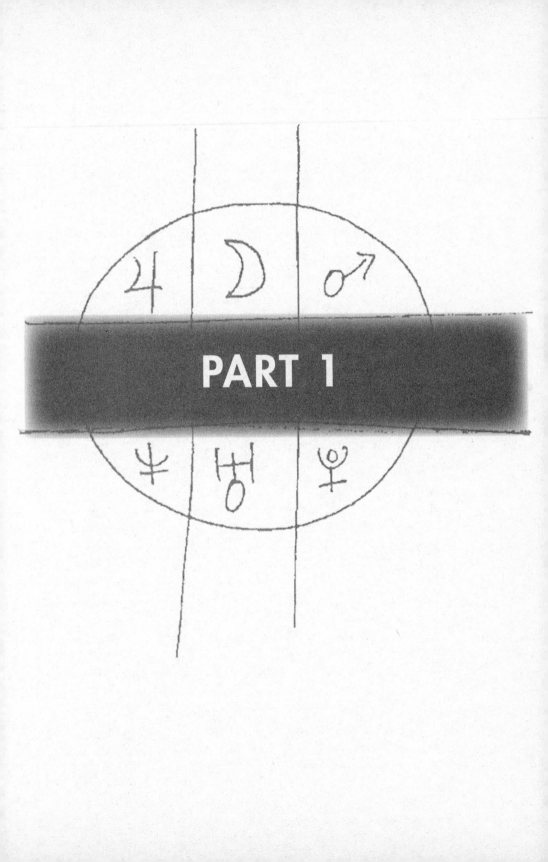

PART 1

The Journalists

THE MYSTERIOUS FRENCH psychic enters the lives of her victims through the mail. For decades, she has seized on the desperation of millions. The lonely. The weak. The elderly. They give her everything. Their trust. Their devotion. And their money.

For many, she became an obsession. It was Maria Duval, they were convinced, who would cure their illnesses. It was Maria Duval, they were convinced, who would bring them much-needed money. And it was Maria Duval, they were convinced, who truly loved and cared about them—often, even more than their own families did. They were captivated by the elusive woman with the piercing gaze, convinced she was the only one left who could help them.

It didn't take us long before we too were captivated by this woman. At the time, we were two twenty-eight-year-old journalists looking for our next story. Instead, we ended up falling down a rabbit hole so deep that we were still trying to get out of it years later.

We were a relatively new investigative duo at CNN. A tall, blond Idaho native who spent years studying Arabic and worked at a newspaper in the Middle East before joining CNN and traveling to North Dakota in an RV to cover the emerging oil boom. And a short brunette from California who studied journalism in the freezing cold of Syracuse, New York, before becoming a local newspaper reporter back in Los Angeles, covering a corrupt city councilman who was later indicted for embezzling thousands of dollars from a local farmers market. Even though we worked for one of the world's largest television news operations, we both considered ourselves more like old-school newspaper reporters than aspiring correspondents.

When Maria came to our attention, it was the fall of 2015. The first Democratic presidential debate had just aired, Hillary Clinton was facing harsh public questioning about her controversial response to the Benghazi attack, and the real estate mogul Donald Trump was just starting to make waves by unexpectedly dominating Republican polls.

We weren't covering any of that. Instead, we'd spent much of the year writing online investigations for CNN, mainly those that exposed how rogue businesses and organizations were taking advantage of consumers. There was the abusive Texas debt-collection firm working for government agencies all over the country that for decades had sat at the center of political scandals. Animal-control agencies that were killing people's dogs over unpaid fines. Small towns threatening residents with jail time over minor offenses like overgrown yards. After all this, we were trying to figure out what to take on next when we remembered that several readers had sent us multiple boxes of junk mail from unscrupulous political groups and charities preying on the elderly. The boxes had sat under our desks for months, next to piles of books, discarded heels, and a yoga mat or two.

We finally had time to take a look. For the better part of a day, we took over our newsroom's large central conference table, covering much of it with the hundreds of mailings we had been sent. Some were from political groups using scare tactics, warning recipients in large type with "URGENT" and "EMERGENCY" notices that if they didn't act now, they could lose their Social Security or Medicare benefits or that the death tax would wipe out all the money they had been hoping to leave their heirs.

We sorted through the pile, finding countless letters from questionable charities seeking money for veterans and starving children abroad. Often these letters contained some sort of "gift," like a one-dollar bill or a cheap plastic alarm clock to lure in their victims. Then we came across something truly bizarre: a letter from a psychic named Patrick Guerin. We were immediately intrigued by its many details and promises—of lottery winnings, luck, and happiness. The sheer weight of the mailing was also impressive, packaged in a sturdy yellow DHL Global Mail envelope that held a multipart letter and DVD accompaniment. Whoever sent this package clearly had made a significant investment to do so. On one side of the cardboard DVD case was an ominous photo of Patrick, a chubby red-cheeked man with wavy brown hair, wearing a polka-dot tie and a bright red pocket square. On the other side was a weighty promise: "The next 5 minutes could change your life for the better." When we put the DVD in our computer, a five minute, 36 second video clip popped up, showing Patrick meeting with an elderly man named Mr. Dubois, who claimed Patrick was the reason he had recently won the lottery. Also enclosed in the mailing was a realistic-looking tabloid newspaper, in which every article just happened to be about Patrick and Mr. Dubois.

"Mr. Dubois Tells His Story," one headline blared across the top of the page. "I contacted Patrick Guerin, not expecting much, and a few weeks later I won 1.2 MILLION DOLLARS at the lottery and ... I THEN WON A CAR."

In the article, Mr. Dubois recounted just how Patrick turned his life around.

> *What happened to me is incredible. Everything was going badly and I was very unhappy. So, I decided to write to Patrick Guerin, even if I didn't expect much to change.... Since then, all my problems have quickly disappeared, one after the other. But what's even more incredible is that only a few weeks after contacting Patrick Guerin I won more than $1.2 million dollars at the lottery, and then I also won a car! It happened like a miracle, to me, who wasn't even expecting anything.*
>
> *What happened to Mr. Dubois? The secret is revealed to you below.*
>
> *Now discover how you can also benefit and have your life change for the better in the coming weeks.*

At the end of the letter was a request for money, along with a separate order form on which recipients were instructed to share their personal information. Sending this form and a check was all it took for someone's life to change forever, the letter claimed.

Our interest was immediately piqued by this rambling letter, the weird film clip, the phony newspaper all about Mr. Dubois, a form of benevolent wizardry known as "white magic," and Patrick's amazing powers. But why would scammers waste their time on such an unsophisticated ploy? How could anyone possibly fall for this?

Our online search for Patrick showed that his letters had been quite effective, raking in millions of dollars. One of the first search results took us to a US Justice Department press release from the year before, announcing its attempt to shut down a number of psychic mailings, including Patrick's. When we downloaded the original government complaint, however, we realized that Patrick was just a sidekick in a much bigger scheme. The real psychic villain, it appeared, was a woman named Maria Duval.

We searched for Maria next. The search results displayed page after page of emotional complaints from people who had been scammed out of their savings. They had received letters from Maria Duval asking for money in exchange for her personal psychic guidance. Even more common were posts from family members searching for answers.

"How can you do this to an elderly person with Alzheimer's?" one woman asked when she discovered that her mother had sent thousands of dollars to Maria. "She is the biggest scam ever, she should be imprisoned immediately so she can die there," wrote another victim, a brain cancer patient who had sent $1,500 in much-needed disability benefits to Maria after being bombarded by what the person described as "panicky" letters demanding $45 twice a month. Another woman was convinced that Maria's letters somehow had disastrous consequences for her good friend. "I have no doubt that her predictions played a roll [sic] in his last weeks of life." And a seventeen-year-old British girl had been found dead in a river in 1998 with a letter from Maria in her pocket. Her mother told a newspaper that her daughter had been corresponding with the psychic for weeks before her death. "Clare used to be a happy girl but she went down hill after getting involved with all this," she said.

Somehow, this simple psychic scam had reached epic proportions.

Many people think of all psychics as frauds, and there are horror stories about people who lost thousands of dollars to storefront psychics or psychic hotlines. But we had never heard of a psychic scam quite like this one, in which fraudsters used the mail to pinpoint vulnerable targets.

To help determine if the scam was as terrible as it seemed, we called the United States Postal Inspection Service, the law enforcement arm of the US Postal Service, which was working in conjunction with the Justice Department to try to shut down the scam. Inspector Clayton Gerber greeted us with a gravelly voice. Clayton, who had been with the agency for more than a decade, had worked on cases involving everything from child pornography to mail scams, and he most notably was a lead investigator on the Stanford investment fraud case that culminated in a 2012 conviction. In that years-long saga, the Postal Inspection Service worked with the Federal Bureau of Investigation, the Securities and Exchange Commission, and the Internal Revenue Service to shut down a Ponzi scheme run by a man named Allen Stanford. Using the mail to help him carry out his massive investment fraud, Stanford convinced tens of thousands of victims that they were investing in an offshore bank with returns that were too good to be true. He was ultimately sentenced to 110 years in prison for stealing billions of dollars over the course of twenty years.

Maria Duval was the new focus of Clayton's attention, and he told us that this operation was in a class all by itself. In fact, he was adamant that it was one of the world's largest and longest-running cons in history, spanning decades and stealing hundreds of millions of dollars. He said he wouldn't be surprised if total losses bordered on $1 billion. "Maria Duval's name comes up in almost every major country," he told us. And then he said something that really threw us for a loop: he had no idea if Maria Duval even existed.

He went on to tell us that this was one of the most frustrating cases he had ever worked on, because of how hindered the US government was by the international scope of this far-reaching scheme, which made it impossible to get to the true source of the letters even after years and years of trying. He said that as investigative journalists, we could break through barriers that he and his colleagues couldn't, so it was crucial for us to pursue the story.

When we hung up, we had far more questions than answers. But one thing was clear: we had found the subject of our next investigation. It was baffling that letters from a psychic had managed to reel in so many victims and alarming that someone was taking advantage of people in their most vulnerable states, and we couldn't help but wonder how many parents and grandparents had been victimized by this—maybe even one of our own.

Over the next months and years, our curiosity would take us on an extraordinary adventure that became darker and more twisted with each corner we turned.

The Promises

Dear [YOUR NAME HERE],

You may have already received the special package I put together for you which contains "Your Special Compendium of Divine Formulas" and your genuine Cross of Invocation of the 7 Powers. Due to the confidential nature of its contents, I felt it necessary to send it to you in a separate package. If you have not yet received it, you should expect to find it in your mailbox in the next couple of days.

As promised, I have completed your first personal astral-clairvoyant forecast for the months to come.

Surprisingly, [YOUR NAME HERE], your case requires more pages than I had anticipated. There are many things I have discovered about you and you are going to learn about them in a few moments.

I have also noted the answer to the question which is bothering you most at this time, the problem being:

Will this nation improve?

Here, soon you are going to learn my answer on this matter. I am also going to give you your personal lucky numbers for the lottery and for other games of chance.

I still have many other facts and events to reveal to you about yourself, [YOUR NAME HERE], and about your future.

Even if it may surprise you for the moment, I have much good news to tell you. But first, I want to ask you to please remember this date (and even to write it down somewhere):

May 2, 2014, [YOUR NAME HERE], as you are going to realize in a moment, May 2, 2014 will mark a very positive turning point in your life. It will be the start of a period that has every chance of being the most important in your entire life.

Unfortunately, I also have some less good news. But please don't worry about it. I am going to show you how to avoid the negative moments, the hurdles and the worries which lie in your path. And even how to turn them to your advantage.

But, before going on, I want to thank you, [YOUR NAME HERE], for having shown confidence in me. I'm going to do EVERYTHING to be of help to you. . . .

[13 pages later]

When, very soon, you already notice the first positive changes in your life . . . When the months pass, you see your life being transformed as you wish it to be . . . When you notice, on your own, that everything I have told you is proven true, you will be delighted you had confidence in me.

You have my solemn word.

Your devoted friend,
Maria Duval

The Scam

WITH CHIN-LENGTH PLATINUM blond hair, dark lips, and a secretive expression on her face, Maria stares directly at her victims through the pages of each letter.

She boasts of her extraordinary powers and worldwide reputation. She claims to have a spiritual gift passed down to her by her uncle, a minister who was heralded as a saint in the small Italian village where he lived. These extraordinary psychic powers, the letters explain, have helped her find countless missing people and catapulted her to international fame.

She tells of books she has written, secret psychic meetings she has led, and thousands of television, radio, and newspaper interviews she has given. She claims that she has provided guidance to Hollywood stars, who pay as much as $700 for a single consultation; several American presidents; and many other political leaders. In fact, she says that many of the world's richest and most famous celebrities never make a decision without consulting her first and that she is the only psychic ever to have been granted an audience with the pope.

Citing all these accomplishments and fame, she tells recipients how lucky they are to have been chosen by her. And the letters really do look handwritten, with notes excitedly scrawled in the margins and circular stains that make it appear she was sipping coffee while writing down her visions.

Filled with personal details from each recipient's life, the letters predict huge lottery winnings and other life-changing events:

Goldie: There are 3, yes <u>THREE</u> Friday the 13ths in 2009. <u>So, 3 opportunities to win a large sum of money!</u> And that's not all: Two of these Friday the 13ths are in <u>consecutive months and they're coming up in just a few weeks: Friday, February 13th and Friday, March 13th!</u> This exceptional phenomenon happens only once every hundred years. There are even many people for whom this will never happen in their lives, but you are one of the lucky ones. Yes, this is going to happen to you Goldie, but <u>only once in your lifetime</u> and it's only a few weeks away!! But first, you must possess the tools and know-how to be able to take advantage of this <u>unique chance</u> which is <u>never, ever</u> going to happen again in your life.

Of course, most people of sound mind would simply dismiss a wild prediction like this. They might even get a good laugh before promptly tossing the letter in the trash, along with credit card offers and other pieces of junk mail. But Maria's letters prey on the very people who no longer have the ability to determine fact from fiction. Many of these victims are battling the crippling mental effects of Alzheimer's disease or dementia, already struggling to remember the people around them or what they ate for breakfast, just as the letters arrive in their mailbox. Others are so lonely and desperate for companionship that they cling to Maria and her promises without thinking twice. Some, who are watching their savings dwindle, are worried about how they'll manage to pay for their last years or whether they'll have anything left to leave behind for their family, so the promise of a windfall is especially tempting.

After reading letters that included such personal details as birthdays, hometowns, and astrological signs, we finally understood how the letters could seem so prescient, especially to people who were already desperate to believe.

You were born under the sign of Taurus. In Chinese astrology, you were born under the sign of the Rabbit. You are mainly under the influence of Venus. In addition, being born on May 22, 1927 in Kansas City, at 12:00 I can already see some aspects of your personality. Like everyone, you have some faults.

Once the specifics about a victim's life are established, letters like this go on to detail personality traits, worries, and regrets that could be helped by Maria.

- *I can also see that you have some great qualities. Among other things, you are generous, sensual and also, sensitive.*
- *I see that, at this time, you are having money problems and you might quickly need $2,500. It's a matter which seems to me very important for you at present. I see such a sum could do a great deal for your happiness. You need more money in order to live in the style you would like, and to be more generous to the people you love.*
- *I can also see other periods of good luck and many opportunities which came your way. Unfortunately, you were unable—or did not wish—to recognize them and grasp them. You simply let them slip away. I can also see several large sums of money which were within your reach, but there again, you were "wearing a blindfold." You ignored the right moments to act. You also started things at the wrong time. I cannot tell you exactly how*

many "only chances" slipped through your fingers, but I can tell you that it was a considerable number over all these years. You missed excellent opportunities which were cast your way ... and which could have changed your future.

These letters are endless. For many recipients, Maria quickly becomes their closest confidant, prompting them to respond with heartfelt letters of their own. Often carefully written in perfect cursive reminiscent of another era, these responses from her elderly victims tell a story of desperation and loneliness, detailing everything from upcoming doctor's visits to growing financial troubles.

In one, dated May 9, 2014, a devoted follower said he was almost brought to tears when he heard from her.

"Something tells me that I can trust you. I almost know how I will feel. I'm already thinking what I would do with ALL this money. The number one thing. My wife would not have to work anymore and would drive a NEWER car. So I would too. We could <u>install</u> AIR CONDITIONING in our house," he wrote, underlining the word "install" for emphasis.

After signing the letter "Your Friend," he scrawled a note at the very bottom of the letter: "I forgot! A <u>good</u> amount of this money would go to the BANK."

Like many others before him, this man didn't realize he was actually just another victim. Maria Duval hadn't been thinking of him. In fact, she had no idea who he was. That supposedly handwritten letter that had brought him to tears? It was one of millions. Other letters just like it had been sent to people all over the United States and the rest of the world, translated into all different languages. And the letter he wrote back—addressed to Maria—was later found in a Dumpster in Long Island, New York. As part of a US government investigation, letters from hundreds of victims were found in this same Dumpster, eventually becoming physical evidence that we were able to read through ourselves, giving us key insight into just how devoted Maria's victims really were.

Investigators also found personal photos and even locks of hair in the Dumpsters, all of which had been requested by Maria's letters as a way to gain psychic contact. The only thing missing were the payments that had been sent with these personal mementos. After all, her advice didn't come free. After she'd hooked victims with her claims of selfless benevolence, they were instructed to send her payments, usually around forty to fifty dollars, in exchange for lucky numbers, specialized guidance, and magic talismans.

In one letter, Maria spends multiple pages describing a magnetized photo of herself, which she says will allow her to establish her "first mediumistic contact" with the lucky recipient. When the magnet is flipped over, a photo of "the most powerful pentacle" appears, which Maria says will ward off misfortune.

> *I am asking you to keep my magnetized talisman on you, or near you, always. (You are going to understand why later.) It is really going to help change your life in a positive way, if you follow the advice I am about to give you. Everyone to whom I've given this magnetized talisman in the past has thanked me.*

Her letters are filled with explanations of charms like this. The thousand-year-old talismans of Love and Luck, which she said had been passed down to her from her grandfather and had helped save one of her own romantic relationships many years ago, and the centuries-old Five Forces Precious Stone, which Maria claims possesses ancient forces that will protect those who wear it from "negative influences" wherever they go. In other letters, she tells of "vibratory crystals" specially marked with each person's name and unique number. She says she received these irreplaceable gems in a secret package and only later learned that her assistant had brought them to her all the way from Paraguay.

> *They are wrenched from the mountains by volcanic eruptions and erosion, falling into rivers where they are sought for their beauty and their "powers." The crystal is a "living" stone that has a heart, a sort of atomic battery, with the power to harness and redirect energy. When you come into contact with this "battery," you feel this mysterious energy penetrate and spread through your body. This pure energy can channel your thoughts and then change the course of events! As soon as you wear your Vibratory Crystal, your mind instantly sharpens, you feel your energy levels surge and you feel charged with renewed strength and the resolve to move mountains! Nothing can stand in your way! You are going to find it easy to harness that strength to get whatever you want from life and resolve all your problems.*

For the millions of people who have sent in money, these talismans have served as physical proof that Maria Duval exists and, more important, that she is looking out for them. From family members, we heard stories of recipients who refused to leave their homes without one of these trusty talismans in their pockets or around their neck. Others couldn't sleep without one under their pillow.

In reality, these "talismans" were pieces of junk, mass-produced in places like China. We later held one of them in our own hands, a flimsy gold disk the size of a coin with a crude angel imprinted on top. It was nothing more than what a quarter might have gotten you as a child from a gas station vending machine. Government investigators found a number of these reportedly magical talismans discarded in those same Long Island Dumpsters outside a business involved with the scheme, some even bearing "Made in China" stickers. They determined that these worthless trinkets had been bought in bulk by the scam's operators and kept on hand en masse to accommodate the demand from victims.

It's almost impossible to find another case of consumer fraud that has touched more people, as many recipients responded to the letters so many times they ended up giving thousands of dollars, wiping out modest monthly Social Security checks, and draining bank accounts. The scam is so widespread that it's hard to know just how many have been affected and just how much money has been stolen. US officials estimate that in the United States and Canada alone, the scheme has raked in more than $200 million from more than 1.4 million victims—a number that is already sixty times the number of victims of the infamous Bernie Madoff Ponzi scheme.

It's unclear when exactly the Maria Duval scam started, but the earliest evidence we found dated it back to the 1980s. Since then, a laundry list of government agencies across the globe have attempted to put an end to it, from the US Department of Justice to the mayor of the tiny town of Wolfurt, Austria.

But somehow, it has raged on for decades.

As investigative reporters, we were typically drawn to corrupt politicians or dangerous criminals. But it was this scam's unbelievable power, which had allowed it to grow so massive and seemingly unstoppable, that hooked us. It was eventually what helped us hook our editors too, convincing them that this was not your average scam. Even then, we knew there must be something bigger at play.

The Victims

I T IS NOT until you meet Maria's victims that her power is truly understood.

And since so few of them even realize they are being deceived, it is often through their family members that their stories are told. Like Doreen Robinson, whose daughter Chrissie gave us a window into how such an unlikely target for this scam ultimately became the perfect victim.

A petite, unassuming woman in her late fifties, with curly blond hair and a charming Canadian accent, Chrissie warmly welcomed us into her adobe-style home facing a canyon of cactus-studded mountains in the heart of Arizona, where she and her husband, Scott, flee to escape the frigid Canadian winters. Sitting nervously across from us at her wooden dining room table, she started the story with the painful final chapter.

By the end, Doreen was on too many medications to remember. There were a couple for her high blood pressure. There were the blood thinners, the shots of vitamin B, and a medication meant to slow down the debilitating disease transforming her into an almost unrecognizable version of herself. In the final stretches, as tears ran down her cheeks and she yelled *"No, no, no!"* over and over again from her nursing home bed, she was prescribed pills for her increasing anxiety and depression. Chrissie would later discover that her mom had begun scribbling "help me, help me, please help me" in barely coherent handwriting deep in the pages of her beloved address book.

In healthier, happier years, Doreen was fiercely independent. Chrissie recalled how Doreen refused to leave the house without the perfect shade of poppy-red lipstick that was always matte, never shiny. In the fall of 2014, she spent her final days lying in a hospital bed dressed in a drab hospital gown. Her face was frighteningly pale and her lips thin and bare. Doreen was in one of fifty rooms in the dementia unit of a Canadian nursing home. Although the room was initially generic and sterile, Chrissie had tried to make it feel more like home. She decorated it with three intricate needlepoints of beautiful angels Doreen had won awards for just years earlier. A calendar sat near her bed that showed each passing day crossed out, along with a collection of books and a smattering of old photos of young Doreen and more recent shots of her and her family. She'd had a strong and feisty personality, but the disease attacking her brain now robbed her of everything that made her the woman she once was. Eventually, Chrissie remembers, it took away even her sense of irony and laughter, leaving "nothing but shadows in her mind's eye that caused her endless anxiety and fear." Most strikingly, her eyes lost any flicker of life, returning the loving looks from her family with a hollow, blank stare.

Just two days before her mother passed away, Chrissie almost thought she saw a flicker of recognition in Doreen's eyes as her family hovered above her bed, talking to her softly and playing soothing sounds of chirping birds, trickling streams, and blowing wind from a CD. And as they tried to grapple with the nurse's prediction that

Doreen likely had only hours, not days, to live, Chrissie wondered whether her mother would prove them all wrong. "Bless her heart, Mum has always liked to be in charge of matters and it wouldn't surprise us if she stubbornly hung on," she wrote in an email to her family later that evening.

Doreen held on long enough to lock eyes with the chaplain who came to her room to pray for her. In those moments, she allowed her granddaughter Chelsea to snuggle up with her in her bed for hours, as Chelsea cried and shared happy memories. They were all crying, comforted by how the horrific confusion that had racked Doreen's brain for so long finally seemed to be loosening its hold. Perhaps the shadows were finally gone. Maybe now, Doreen could find peace.

The next morning, a nurse came to the room to begin the process of removing Doreen's hydration drip—essentially starving her of the water she would need to continue living. Part of Chrissie was relieved that she was able to see her mother once more. But her heart also ached at the thought of Doreen's body, abandoned by her mind long ago, continuing to fight for much longer. Her muscles were already beginning to jerk and spasm as they reacted to the lack of water and nutrients. So Chrissie carefully crawled into her mother's hospital bed, laid her head beside Doreen's and her arm across her body, and spoke softly through her tears, begging her to let go.

"I finally got up the courage to tell Mum what a wonderful life she'd had, the great plans she'd made for her golden years, and how tortured these past few years had been for her. I urged her to meet her maker, go on to greener pastures."

Within hours, she did. Doreen passed away on September 20, 2014, at four p.m. with her two sons beside her, on a warmer-than-usual 60 degree day in September. All the machines attached to Doreen's crumbling body were removed, and she finally looked at peace.

Chrissie, who of Doreen's children lived the farthest away, had left her mother's bedside and was in her yard gardening when she got the news. "I answered the phone and my world crumbled in what I knew was coming." Chrissie was told that her mother's official cause of death was heart failure.

Ten days later, at Doreen's funeral, Chrissie stood in the same church her mother had joined after immigrating to Canada half a century earlier. Chrissie remembers that she wore dark gray slacks and a black knit cowl-neck sweater that hid a bloodred shirt underneath, and she recited an emotional eulogy remembering her mother and sharing memories of the battle with Alzheimer's disease that had caused her family so much heartbreak.

Two years after her mother's death, Chrissie's eyes darted around and occasionally filled with tears as she searched for the right words to tell us about her mother and her final years. It was during this dark, downward spiral that her mother had lost her radiant smile. Her head filled with inescapable demons. This was the same time when she was ultimately dragged into an obsession that Chrissie will never forget, one that took over much of Doreen's final years.

. . .

Chrissie will never be sure when exactly her mother got her first letter from Maria Duval or how she became a target.

What she does know is that in the months leading up to her mother's eightieth birthday, before Chrissie or even Doreen realized that Alzheimer's disease was slowly and silently infiltrating her once rational mind, Doreen had handwritten at least forty different checks in response to Maria's letters, which Doreen believed were ending up with the psychic.

Chrissie suspects that her mother's obsession with these letters had far more to do with gambling on a cure for her failing mind than with winning a financial jackpot. In fact, Chrissie would later find evidence of an internal battle that Doreen hid from her children for years. She'd kept a *Reader's Digest* book full of brain games promising to keep her mind sharp. Not a single page was completed. Chrissie also found scribbled and practically nonsensical attempts to document Doreen's early years in England, unfinished needlepoints that once would have been simple for Doreen to complete, and a small personal address book in which her inner demons leaped from the page. In one place, she incorrectly wrote her son's phone number over and over again. In another, she wrote in misspelled fragments of being quarantined in her room at the assisted living facility due to a virus that had broken out there, and how she desperately hoped to get out. On other pages, she furiously wrote her son's name repeatedly, sometimes followed by the words, "I kneed [*sic*] new shoes," and "Help me."

"You could see the pressure of the pen. Obviously she was angry with herself," Chrissie said. "To have a glimpse into somebody's mind like that—how difficult it was for her to figure out a phone number that she has phoned for so many years. It's scary."

We leafed through the pages of this small book as we talked to Chrissie. And though we had never met Doreen, it was painful for us to read these outbursts from a woman so trapped in her own mind.

But this all came later. The first time Chrissie began to realize how bad things had gotten was in the winter of 2010, when she helped her mother go through all the paperwork that had been building up in the condo where Doreen lived alone.

It was all so out of character. Doreen was once frugal and practical to a fault, owning her own successful business and managing her family's finances at a time when few women did so. Now she seemed to have become an entirely different person. Doreen's children found buried within the piles of coupons, magazines, junk mail, and the occasional misplaced sock a bill from a department store credit card with a shockingly high balance. Concerned, Chrissie dug into the rest of her mother's finances. And when she turned to her mother's bank statements, she saw a disturbing number of payments to two names she didn't recognize: Destiny Research Center (while this name would remain a mystery to Chrissie, it would become very important to us) and Maria Duval. Every check was made for the same precise amount of $59 (in Canadian dollars).

"Who is this? What is this place? What are you getting for this money?" Chrissie asked her mother.

Suddenly, her mother's pleasant demeanor was gone. She turned defensive and secretive and simply shrugged in response to Chrissie's questions and admonishments. "She was unable— not unwilling, but unable—to specify what she was getting in return for this amount of money," Chrissie remembers. "She finally showed me large round metal talismans encased in little velveteen pouches with symbols and some with motivational words or astrological signs on them."

These talismans must have been in her mother's home for months. Only after this realization did Chrissie begin to notice them everywhere she looked, tucked away among her mother's valued possessions. In her jewelry chest and dresser drawers, under papers, and in her purse. She even remembers Doreen wearing one around her neck. One time, when Chrissie was trying to tidy up the dresser in Doreen's bedroom, she noticed a velvet pouch with a flimsy medallion inside it.

"I shook it out and said, 'Oh, what's this? Is it garbage?' I remember her taking it from me and clasping it in her hands, saying, 'No, no, that's special' and putting it back into that pouch and holding that pouch like there was no way she was going to let me take that."

It was soon evident to Chrissie that the cheap trinkets and the mysterious woman from the letters were an inescapable presence in her mother's life.

When Doreen was at her best, Chrissie convinced her that the letters were a terrible scam that was stealing her retirement savings. This realization took a huge toll on Doreen. "She was shocked, dismayed, and ashamed when she realized her stupidity and the financial damage she'd caused herself," Chrissie said. "I gave Mum strict orders to throw away anything from Maria Duval or Destiny Research; she seemed to understand my frustration and anger [at this scam] and readily agreed."

Still, as her memory declined, Doreen turned into a Dr. Jekyll of sorts and quickly returned to her secretive relationship with Maria, almost like a child hiding a secret stash of candy from her parents. Even after Chrissie and her brothers took away Doreen's checkbooks and assumed legal responsibility for her finances, she would cobble together piles of cash and coins to make up the amount Maria was requesting from her.

In a call that Chrissie will always remember, a woman named Maryanne, who worked as the secretary for her mother's financial adviser, told Chrissie she needed to drive to Doreen's house immediately. Maryanne explained that Doreen had called her earlier, telling her through tears that she had "done something naughty." When Maryanne had arrived, she'd found Doreen surrounded by envelopes addressed to scammers like Maria Duval and stuffed with cash and coins. Doreen was completely distraught. After hurrying over, Chrissie walked into a heartbreaking scene, with Maryanne counting and sorting the money as Doreen sat looking on. "Mum wrung her hands, sitting forlornly in her armchair, a stack of tissues in her lap."

This incident proved to Chrissie just how much Doreen was wrapped up in the scam. From two years' worth of bank statements, she's certain that Doreen sent at least $2,400 to the psychic. Her total losses were likely much larger.

"These scammers seem to have targeted my mother as easy prey, probably from the very first check she sent to them," Chrissie told us. "Not only was my poor mother quickly losing her mind due to Alzheimer's disease, she was lonely, bored, [and] wanting to be wealthy and well. She didn't have the quality of mind anymore to *realize* how much money she was losing or how *often* she was sending money!"

Finally, knowing that the painful tug-of-war with her mother wasn't going to get her anywhere, Chrissie turned her anger and frustration to Maria. She reported the crime to the police, but they told her there was little they could do to help recover any of the money Doreen had given away. So she sent letter after letter to the address on the solicitations, tersely demanding a refund ("of any amount—even just $59.00 to show good faith") and for Doreen's name to be stripped from the mailing list. Her efforts proved fruitless. So Chrissie's brother finally resorted to forwarding Doreen's mail to his own home, where he could sort through all the junk mail and scam letters, keeping only the bills and other important documents. At one point, he received thirty-six scam letters in a single day, all addressed to Doreen. As his trash soon overflowed with her mail, Doreen was crestfallen by her suddenly empty mailbox.

Doreen's relationship with Maria had clearly taken over much of her life. It was Maria, it seemed, who helped her get through some of her loneliest days. The psychic's lengthy, personalized letters with all of their promises gave her something to look forward to—and hope that her life, and especially her health, could change for the better.

So as Chrissie's brother handled all the mail, Chrissie turned into an armchair detective, scouring the internet in an attempt to uncover which heartless criminals had gotten their hands on her mother's hard-earned money.

"It was painful. Then it was frustrating. Then I just grew angry," Chrissie said. "I'm not an angry person by any means. It takes a lot to get me mad but, boy oh boy, to find out how long they had taken advantage of this woman who believed that she was getting something for her money."

Chrissie spent months trying to get to the bottom of the fraud. When her mother passed away a few years later, roughly a year before we began our own hunt for answers, Chrissie still had no idea who was behind the Maria Duval letters.

· · ·

Maria's letters weren't the only ones that enthralled Doreen.

As her mind deteriorated, she descended into an alternate universe in which her daily pile of mail became what she lived for. In these piles she found exciting, official-looking letters telling her that she was the lucky winner of thousands of dollars, mail-order catalogs with colorful photos of nifty gadgets that she could look forward to arriving on her doorstep, and pages and pages of thoughtful and uplifting letters from her pen pal Maria Duval.

In her right mind, Doreen would have kept only what was important, like a letter from a friend, a financial statement from a bank, or a Christmas card from a family member. As her condition worsened, everything blended together. It was nearly impossible to sort the truth from the lies. She didn't realize that the official-looking notices promising lottery winnings, for instance, were nothing more than phony award templates designed on someone's computer and that she was not a lucky winner. She also didn't realize that the money she was sending in to claim these prizes would be lost forever.

In the winter of 2010, when her children found that first department store credit card bill hidden in the clutter that covered much of her home, they also discovered that all these scams and mail-order purchases had dug their mother into tens of thousands of dollars of debt. Adding it up by hand, Chrissie determined that Doreen owed more than $50,000 to four different credit card companies and that for months her primary bank account had been overdrafted. As a result, they were forced to cash out a chunk of Doreen's prized retirement savings to keep her from spiraling even deeper into this hole.

Even as her family tried to rein her in, one of her sons caught her with two envelopes waiting to be mailed, filled with ninety dollars apiece, addressed to a place in Malaysia. Another time, Doreen was stopped just before sending even more money to mailboxes in New York and elsewhere overseas. In Doreen's mind, these payments would allow her to receive large sums of money that were on hold just for her.

Doreen's story didn't come as a surprise to us. Our investigation into this shadowy world of mail fraud would show us that elderly people around the world, a generation that has traditionally trusted what reached them through mail delivered by government postal workers, were the prime targets of scams like the Maria Duval letters. Many of them are desperate to believe the outlandish claims of huge winnings, better health, or companionship. They give away their life savings as they respond to letter after letter, scam after scam. One of the readers who sent us the piles of scam letters and solicitations told us the story of her relative, who drained the entire $100,000 reverse mortgage on her house, forcing her into her worst nightmare as she lived out her final years in a nursing home. Each of these heartbreaking stories adds up to a staggering amount of damage to a segment of society that can afford it the least, with elderly Americans losing around $3 billion to fraud and other financial abuses every year.

In many cases, this financial ruin starts with what is known as a "sucker list." Someone may give a generous donation to a charity, respond to a newspaper advertisement for a supposed research study, or buy a magazine from Publisher's Clearing House in the hopes of winning big. But then his or her name becomes currency, often starting out with some legitimate business or nonprofit but soon ending up with professional data and list brokers who may be willing to sell such names to anyone who will buy them.

These lists of names, bundled in categories like elderly lottery players, technologically challenged, and likely to believe in psychics, are big business in the world of scammers. They are what make it possible for even the most amateur con artist to reach an astounding number of victims, and specifically to target the people who will be most vulnerable to his or her schemes—people like Doreen.

Chrissie has no idea how her mother landed on one of these lists, whether it was through subscriptions to *Reader's Digest*, Publisher's Clearing House, or some other random mail-order purchase. All she knows is that somehow her mother was directly in the crosshairs.

Amid all the different scams that entered Doreen's mailbox over the years, Maria Duval's was something special. Doreen couldn't even explain it to Chrissie when she asked her about it. There was something that kept Doreen sending check after check, even as she could barely fill out the boxes and sign her own name.

· · ·

Maria's victims are all over the world, but they have one thing in common: desperation. We found stories from her victims everywhere we looked—online, in old newspaper clippings, and in the many government documents detailing the scam.

Many of the victims reminded us of Doreen: Suffering from illnesses that were chipping away at their brains. Lonely after spouses and friends had passed away. Living on a fixed income and worried about everyday bills or the money they were going to be able to leave behind. "He is so desperate for money that he pins all his hopes on this," one person wrote online about their ninety-six-year-old father-in-law who refused to believe that the letters were a scam and even tried to send a cash payment after his family closed his bank account.

In a letter to Maria that was found by US authorities, another victim wrote that she was in such serious financial straits that she was struggling to afford new glasses or a dentist appointment. She apologized to Maria for not writing more often, telling her that she was "in distress" with back problems. "I am getting more broke every day. I can't send what I don't have."

And an eighty-two-year-old widow from Oregon said she regretted the day she first sent money to Maria. Even after realizing it was a scam, she wrote in a 2009 complaint that money continued to be deducted from her checking account—presumably because the scammers had access to her account and were making automatic deductions. "I live on Social Security, so don't have very much money. Can someone please help me?" she wrote.

It was clear that people like this were the perfect targets. But we wanted to understand why. So we called Dr. Peter Lichtenberg, a clinical psychologist and the director of Wayne State University's Institute of Gerontology, who has studied the financial exploitation of the elderly and the underlying psychology of scams for years.

"It's a combination of loneliness, depression, and a real sense of invisibility," he told us when we asked him what made people fall for a scam like the Maria Duval letters. This isolation and psychological vulnerability creates the perfect setting for a scammer to enter people's lives. As they are feeling invisible to society and even to their own families, suddenly someone out there—in this case, a woman who looks so trustworthy and kind from her photo alone—has chosen them and is giving them the attention they have been missing. For those who feel like they have lost their sense of self, this scam makes them feel important. The promises of financial windfalls also tap into the overwhelming desire at this stage in people's lives to be able to create a legacy for future generations.

To make matters worse, many people suffering from dementia are more likely to become secretive or suspicious of their own family members, especially if those individuals are attempting to pry into their finances or personal lives. This makes someone like Maria, whose letters profess love for who they are and an understanding of everything they're going through, that much more attractive. And it makes it even harder for families to break through. The Maria Duval scam reminds Dr. Lichtenberg of a cult in the way that it creates a special relationship with its victims that is entirely resistant to logic.

"The key is almost cult indoctrination. . . . They're so far in, you have to cut the contact off in order for them to come back to reality," he said. "It's the leader, the belief in this person, in this woman and her magical gifts and her specialness."

Hearing this, we thought about how family members told us about letters warning victims to keep their relationship with Maria a secret, one that outsiders simply wouldn't understand. Dr. Lichtenberg said that even mild symptoms of aging can affect someone's ability to reason—a person doesn't need to have severe cognitive impairment. Deteriorating memories can also play a role in an individual's susceptibility to such a scam, as many victims are unable to estimate just how much money they've been sending.

Some of Maria's victims weren't elderly or cognitively impaired at all. Rather, they were simply lonely, and looking for a last resort. And others just seemed more easily persuadable, trusting to a fault. "I have sent this woman lots of my money where I could not pay my bills," a mother of five wrote in an online consumer complaint forum in 2014, saying that she was living on a fixed income and thought that sending money to Maria would help bring about a better life for her children. "Yes I feel like a fool, but when you receive [these] letters over and over you feel like a failure if you did not send it in to get a better life for your children." In another online complaint, a woman from Michigan recounted how Maria's letters had come to her in some of her darkest days—soon after she separated from her husband, lost her job, and said a hard goodbye to her son, who had joined the military. "This scam crushed the last bit of hope I had in any kindness or miracle that could be, and pushed me over the edge," she wrote. "Congrats! You got another weak one."

A Utah resident ended up in even worse financial shape after sending money to Maria. "All she wanted from me is money. Now I am homeless and $5000.00 in debt," the person wrote in an online complaint. "I need dental care, and I have no money to pay."

It wasn't surprising for Dr. Lichtenberg to hear that it wasn't just

the elderly who were being duped by this scam. The same desperation can attack anyone's judgment, he told us, whether someone is
dealing with a death in the family, job loss, financial misfortune, or
depression. "The human condition is not all that different throughout life," he said. "People get the feeling of invisibility and think, 'This
is not what life should be, this is not what I expected life to be.'"

In some cases, Maria's letters have taken a more sinister tone,
suggesting that misfortune awaited those who ignored her.

In 1997, one woman told the Scottish *Sunday Mail* newspaper
that she was terrified of what would happen if she didn't send
money. "When I wrote to say I didn't have that kind of cash, the letters got even more frightening," she said at the time. "I was so scared
I couldn't eat or sleep, worrying whether I'd be hit by more bad
luck."

Dr. Lichtenberg said that scare tactics like this can be incredibly
effective, and in many cases they are employed as a last resort to get
a victim's money. "It's all sweet and nice as long as the cash is coming, and if that stops it can get very dark," he told us. "The path of
least resistance is to just send more money."

Listening to Dr. Lichtenberg talk, we realized that this scam
truly used every tool in the book. Other popular schemes seemed to
rely on one main emotion. Schemes promising lottery wins rely on
hope. Romance scams, in which fraudsters develop fake relationships with victims, rely on loneliness. And so-called grandparent
scams that convince family members to wire money to a loved one
they claim is in crisis rely on fear. But Maria's letters use a combination of all these emotions.

This is what made the scam so powerful. The letters appealed to
the most base emotions of fear, loneliness, and hope—making it
nearly impossible for victims to resist.

• • •

The most tragic story we encountered was that of the young British girl who reportedly drowned with Maria's letter in her pocket. She was only seventeen years old at the time of her death.

Found screaming for help as she was subsumed into the river Wear in Sunderland, a city in northeast England, Clare Ellis ventured into the water on a cold December night in 1998 for unclear reasons. "When we arrived she was still alive and shouting, but we couldn't find any ropes long enough to reach her and there weren't any lifebelts," police constable Kim Maynard told a newspaper reporter at the time. Maynard reportedly jumped into the rushing water in an attempt to save the girl, but she was already unconscious. "I managed to get hold of her and started pulling her in, but by that stage she had stopped shouting and I couldn't feel a pulse."

Maynard, a thirty-eight-year-old father of two, told reporters that the water was so cold that it took the wind out of him. He used a lifeboat to bring her to shore, where he attempted to resuscitate her. But it was too late. After being rushed to the hospital, she was pronounced dead a few hours later.

In the wake of Clare's death, which media reports said the coroner ruled the result of hypothermia, her parents were curious about what had driven their daughter into the water that night. Her mother had a disturbing theory.

"She was writing to a psychic woman. She said the woman had magical powers," she told a reporter, suggesting that letters from this psychic had pushed her daughter over the edge. Her parents told reporters that over the past few months, Clare had become uncharacteristically fixated on all kinds of clairvoyants, and that she had recently secured a new job at a clothing factory that they'd hoped would help take her mind off this newfound obsession.

In the days, weeks, and months that followed her drowning, newspapers and tabloids across the United Kingdom pounced on the story, with headlines ranging from sensational to heartless:

DEAD TEENAGER'S PSYCHIC FIXATION

RIDDLE OF DROWNING 'SPIRITGIRL'

RIVERDEATH GIRL IN PSYCHIC RID

It was an article from a few years later that eventually zeroed in on Maria Duval as the psychic from the letters. "In Clare's pocket was a letter from French psychic Maria Duval, to whom she had been writing in the weeks leading up to her death," reported an article in the *Evening Chronicle*.

Clare's mother told the paper that her daughter had "spent a fortune" on Maria's talismans and that her behavior was becoming more and more concerning. She was convinced that the psychic's unshakable grip on Clare had played a role in her death. "These things just shouldn't be allowed," she said. "We even got letters from this woman for months after Clare had died. Clare used to be a happy girl but she went down hill after getting involved with all this."

The Address

Maria Duval
c/o Destiny Research Center
1285 Baring Blvd., #411
Sparks, NV 89434-8673

On the surface, the obscure address to which victims from all over the United States had once been directed to send their money appeared to be the address of an actual person.

No. 411 could be a unit in a retirement village or apartment building. Some quick research on Sparks would show that it was a middle-income town just down the highway from the casinos of Reno, where retirees flock for cheap gambling. It's no wonder someone might believe Maria herself was opening each of his or her heartfelt letters and handwritten checks from her own home there.

The image of Maria unsealing each envelope from her living room, looking through each person's letters, photos, and locks of requested hair, helped her build trust and a personal connection to her victims. Some of them even sent her Christmas gifts every year, along with long, handwritten notes that they hoped would give Maria a window into their lives.

It was later, after we'd first written about the scam, that a woman told us that her elderly father had been convinced that Maria was his pen pal. "The letters my father received were directed at his loneliness after the passing of my mother," she wrote. "They implied a 'relationship' between my father and 'Maria.' . . . When I discussed this with my dad he was under the impression that it was a 'nice woman who lived in Nevada' [Sparks] who he was getting to know, through letters. . . . My dad isn't tech savvy so they were 'pen pals.'"

Smart enough to know that this was a scam and furious at whoever was taking advantage of her father, the woman was determined to hold him or her accountable. She thought she would finally have the opportunity when she arrived in Reno on a business trip.

"I actually did some research and found a street address in Sparks and attempted to confront these predators," she said. "However the street address led me to an industrial park, with no clear address that I could find. My GPS navigation was telling me I had reached my destination while I was in a desert[-like] area where there were no building [sic]. I asked a few business people in that area, they were of no help, although they did say I wasn't the first to come looking."

We later retraced her steps ourselves, looking for anyone who had heard of this "nice woman from Nevada" and any clues to how this elusive French psychic was connected to this random American town.

From the Reno-Tahoe airport, with its schizophrenic mix of cheesy slot machines and rustic grizzly bear statues, it was only a ten-minute drive to Sparks. A highway filled with semitrucks cut through a flat, barren landscape with the occasional casino, Holiday Inn, or Denny's popping up into the sky. A deserted water park welcomed us off the freeway. From there, the streets started to look less desertlike, full of planted trees and grass lawns outside generic, modest-size homes.

Our GPS directions took us closer to our ultimate destination than they had apparently taken the woman from the email, yet we still ended up in the middle of a run-down, yellowing strip mall surrounded by small, dusty brown mountains that looked nothing like the beautiful, snow-capped mountains around nearby Lake Tahoe.

MetroPCS. Heroes Games and Hobbies. The Dawg Wash. PJ's Discount Liquor. PC Service Center. A dark unit that we discovered was a church after peeking in the window. And a storefront simply labeled "Mattress."

None of these businesses were located at the specific address we were looking for, but we decided to pop our heads in anyway and ask whether any of the store owners or employees had ever been asked about or heard of a woman named Maria Duval.

As the sounds of off-key horns and loud drums from a marching band practicing at the high school across the street combined with angry rap music blaring from a car in the parking lot, we entered the game and hobby shop. Behind a computer, a red-haired man in glasses looked at us skeptically as we approached—two women in our late twenties who didn't exactly look like gaming aficionados.

When we asked him if anyone had come into his store looking for a woman named Maria Duval, he barely looked up from his screen and gave a small shrug. "People don't come here looking for people," he said, looking around at the war games (think Dungeons & Dragons and Magic) and intricate model kits on the shelves around us. "I really wouldn't have noticed something like that—it's not in my realm of interest."

Next, in PJ's Discount Liquor, a man with piercing eyes looked down at the clock on his cell phone and told us no one had come in looking for Maria other than us—at least since eleven that morning.

The MetroPCS store was closed, and the mattress store was by appointment only. But at the Farmers Insurance office nearby, a friendly-looking man sat at the front desk. When we warned him we had a peculiar question for him, he replied, "It wouldn't be my first today."

He looked a lot like your stereotypical insurance agent: smiling and balding with a bushy gray mustache. And he was the first person who was genuinely intrigued by why we were there. He said that unfortunately he hadn't heard of Maria, and that he would have remembered that name, making an eerie UFO-like sound for effect. When we told him he wasn't too far off with that sound—that she was supposedly a French psychic—he joked, "Well, she would know you're looking for her then."

After hearing our explanation of the scam, he told us that his wife worked at a nearby credit union and often tried to intervene when she suspected elderly customers were withdrawing large amounts of money to send to scammers. "It's tragic that people fall for that stuff. . . . They should bet on me instead. I could sell them life insurance." With life insurance, at least they'd be guaranteed a payout, he explained.

After the cheery insurance agent, we were met with mostly confused looks from employees at the other nearby stores. A wiry-looking middle-aged woman at an eye doctor and glasses shop barely listened to our question before giving us a curt no. A man at the dry cleaner's carrying a pile of clothes on hangers also hadn't heard of Maria. A cluttered computer repair shop transported us back to the 1980s. It was stuffed with outdated monitors, and cheap advertisements were painted on its windows, along with an American flag. We shuffled up to the register and stood near what looked like a high schooler with a backpack who was waiting on some sort of repair. When we asked the owner about Maria, he said he had never heard of her, and that his store had been around for thirteen years.

The employees at an Asian restaurant with a generic sign, tinted windows, and a confused mixture of cuisines were the most curious about our inquiry. "Why does that name sound so familiar? Is she that missing girl?" asked a young female employee wearing a black restaurant tee.

Standing next to her, the heavily tattooed Hawaiian sushi chef was more eager to tell us about how the restaurant would soon become the venue for the first competition of dancing sushi chefs in the area, featuring deep house music and island reggae. A man eating lunch at the counter looked at us quizzically when we explained that we were journalists looking into a scam. Then he asked, "Do you guys dress the same, as reporters?"

Confused, we looked each other up and down and started laughing. Somehow, we had chosen almost identical outfits—denim button-downs with straight black pants and ankle boots. We hadn't noticed until this inquisitive sushi eater pointed it out. If there was a reporter uniform, we were both definitely wearing it.

Getting back to the task at hand, we explained to everyone in the room that an address in this very shopping center had once been used by a psychic scammer under the name "Maria Duval" and that this scam had stolen hundreds of millions of dollars from mainly elderly victims.

"Why Sparks, Nevada? How random is that? It is a little F-ing town," said the same female employee, who wore dark eye makeup, her hair in a ponytail, and chipped red nails. She said the only reason she lived in Sparks was because her kids were there. "She must have known someone here." Before we left, she warned us not to continue our hunt once it got dark—especially without a knife or a large can of Mace (which, conveniently, she said we could buy at a store across the street for eight dollars).

Two doors down from the dancing sushi chef was a small UPS Store. This must have been where all the letters had been going. We entered the one-room office and quickly noticed rows of gold mailboxes tucked away in the back corner. Trying to avoid detection, we walked casually past the employee standing near the store's entrance and tried to quickly spot mailbox 411 or 409 (the two different numbers that appeared with Maria Duval's supposed address on the letters).

401, 402, 403, 404, 405, 406, 407, 408. Then the numbers stopped.

As we craned our heads to see if we had somehow missed another row, a gruff female employee with shoulder-length brown hair and blunt bangs came over and asked us what mailbox we were looking for.

Upon hearing our reply, she quickly turned away and went back to what she had been doing, telling us under her breath that the boxes hadn't been in operation for more than a year and a half, after the store had gotten a notice telling them they would be closed. This made sense to us, since the US government had attempted to put a stop to all of Maria Duval's US mailings a couple of years earlier as part of the Justice Department's lawsuit. She gruffly told us we would need a subpoena to ask any more questions (which suggested to us that the store probably had been subpoenaed about this before).

We tried to explain that we were most interested in hearing about the kinds of people who had come to her store to try to find Maria herself. The employee wasn't moved. In her efforts to try to get rid of us, though, she did let it slip that a few people (who she said were neither old nor young) had come looking. "They just wanted to meet her," she said with a shrug.

We asked her the same question in different ways over and over. We had come so far and hadn't expected to be showed out the door this quickly. But the woman and even her more cheerful coworker manning the front desk both refused to let us talk to the owner, whom we could see huddled in a back room just a few steps away staring at a computer screen, clearly hearing our inquiries but choosing to ignore them. The woman muttered to her boss in a snarky tone, "I told you, they don't listen." Frustrated, we left the store without any answers.

Sparks was just the beginning of a very complicated trail meant to hide the true origins of these letters. In fact, the documents from the US government's investigation revealed that these mailboxes had been opened years earlier, not by Maria Duval, but by a businessman all the way from Switzerland.

Why did he choose Sparks? Nobody knows.

The Mysterious Psychic

S O MARIA DEFINITELY wasn't a "nice woman" living in dusty Sparks, Nevada. But was she a real woman somewhere?

We started with the basics. A simple Google search revealed a number of women named Maria Duval: A German pop singer whose record covers from the 1960s and 1970s show a young brunette woman with a bouffant hairdo. A Mexican actress in her seventies and an elderly Argentine actress who had appeared in more than twenty movies throughout the 1940s. The mentions of these other Maria Duvals were merely sprinkled among the large volume of search results that pertained to the Maria Duval we were looking for.

At the top of the list of websites, blogs, and scam alerts was a jumbled Wikipedia entry that contained a smattering of supposed personal details. It stated that Maria's real name was Carolina Maria Gambia and that she had been born in Milan, Italy, before moving to France. She had a son named Antoine Palfroy, and she was the president of the Institute for Parapsychological Research in the small French town of Callas. The page also provided a potential theory about the letters. It said that Maria had once owned a company called Astroforce, which continued to use her name for the well-known scam "with her consent and knowledge." It stated that she worked in conjunction with Destiny Research Center, the name from the Sparks mailing address and the name Chrissie was so puzzled by.

We would later turn back to this Wikipedia entry, surprised at the glimmers of truth hiding in it. But at the time, we suspected that much of it was nonsense. The Institute for Parapsychological Research? It doesn't exist. And we couldn't find anyone in Italy—or anywhere else, for that matter—with the name Carolina Maria Gambia.

After some more digging, we found a four-person private investigation firm from Calgary, Alberta, called Rainbow Investigations, which appeared to have done some research on Maria. The owner, Ron Reinhold, spent much of his time chasing down cheating spouses and helping businesses screen potential employees. In his spare time, he wrote warnings to the public about insidious consumer frauds. We emailed him to set up an interview once we'd read through his lengthy write-up on the Maria Duval letters. He quickly replied, telling us he'd be happy to talk but would first have to dig up the dossier on the scam he had created and tucked away years ago.

We got on the phone with him the next day. With a distinctly Canadian accent, Ron told us how his fascination with Maria had begun after being contacted by the family of one of her victims. He faxed us all the documents in his file, which included one of the more ominous letters we had seen to date. Featuring graphic photos of a car that had been totaled in a crash, Maria explained in the letter that only her special talismans could protect people from imminent dangers like this.

> *I was involved in a horrible car accident. I got out unharmed while the car was completely destroyed (as you can see on the photograph that I've enclosed with this letter). I am certain I would no*

longer be in this world if it weren't for the Ring of Re. I felt as though it was protecting me.

Ron was also one of the first people we discovered who was convinced that Maria was indeed a real person, though he suspected that she could have died many years ago. "She's not gonna be a young woman if she's still around," he told us.

After our conversation with him, we realized that he wasn't the only one confident in her existence. In archived news articles, journalists had reported that Maria was a real psychic, holed away in the south of France. "The elusive clairvoyant refused requests for an interview, but we can reveal she lives near glamorous St Tropez in a luxury chateau in the village of Callas," one Scottish newspaper wrote in 1997.

Victims of the scam, meanwhile, continued to believe she was real and cursed her online. Among all the angry rants, a few people wrote that they were not only convinced that there was a woman named Maria Duval out there, but that she had helped them win money or improve their lives.

Others at least *hoped* she could be the real deal. "Since I do not have any proof that she is a scam, I do not believe in 'false hopes' as of yet," one person had written almost a decade earlier in an online forum called Astrocat. Dedicated to the Maria Duval letters and other mail scams, this forum was full of conspiracy theorists, all with their own ideas of who Maria was and where the letters were coming from. Many of these commenters were adamant that only suckers would fall for the idea that this woman was actually real. Some, for example, were convinced that the letters all came from a Singaporean man named Tony. Others argued that letters actually pictured an elderly Argentine man in drag.

We were also intrigued to see the sheer number of posts from people who had the very same questions we did.

> Have any considered the possibility that this naria [*sic*] duval business might be part of the business operations of the real criminal organistations [*sic*]? That is the same organisations who deal with drugs, smuggling, stealing, etc.

> What is up with the Maria Duval entity? This is not one person. I keep getting mail from this outfit chronicling my continued bad luck, UNLESS, I send Maria a check to hold for me. How can this kind of fraud continue, unchecked? I haven't sent a penny, nor will I. However, the letters get gloomier and more depressing. . . . The letters emanate bad vibes, if you will. Done in a boiler room.

Some of the implausible theories and clues posted on forums like Astrocat would become important later. At the moment, all the varying accounts only had us confused.

International investigators, whom we corresponded with via email after reading about their efforts online, couldn't help us. Despite all their attempts to shut down the scam, they still didn't know who Maria Duval really was—or if she existed at all.

"She's a glamorous European blonde who claims to see the future and has been published in newspapers worldwide. Problem is, she does not exist," a journalist wrote in 2001, reporting on the New Zealand government's efforts to expose the scam. Three years later, one of the world's largest cross-border agencies, the International Consumer Protection and Enforcement Network, described Maria as a "probably fictitious" character when European members led a 2004 effort to shut down her advertisements and mailings in nine man who was Wolfurt's mayor at the time the letters were just starting to catch the attention of authorities. In his response, he described a situation very similar to the mailboxes in Sparks, Nevada. "Many people of hole [sic] Europe contacted my office wondering if Mrs. Duval is a real person and if she's living here. I had to explain that she never lived her [sic] and I never met her," the former mayor wrote to us. He told us that when he investigated the letters, he discovered that a direct marketing company had used a mailbox in the town's post office, but once the letters garnered some attention, the box had soon been closed. "Now, I'm retired as a Mayor since 6 years and I'm not astonished, that Duval is still working on," he said.

A decade after these many investigations abroad, US officials were also at a loss. As they scrutinized the thousands of letters being sent out with Maria Duval's name and image and counted the millions of dollars lost to the scam, they couldn't figure out whether the photo of the striking blond woman with the secretive smile was anything more than a stock image. "It is unclear whether Maria Duval is a real person, or a fictitious character," US prosecutors said in 2014 court filings.

All these investigations from around the world reached the same dead end. We spent a full week focused on nothing but researching Maria and couldn't find a single government agency that had ever spoken to this woman or even been able to locate her for questioning. Instead, all we found were competing theories, stalled investigations, and generic mailboxes being used as some kind of front.

We had never embarked on an investigation like this. Usually, there was an obvious "bad guy." In this case, we started out thinking that it was Maria. But we still hadn't found any proof that this woman was anything more than a photo used over and over again.

countries. This organization set its sights on stopping the ope
as complaints poured in from all over Europe claiming that 1
were being sent from Maria Duval and another known alias, 1
France. "These probably fictitious names raise false hopes of m
tunate and wretched individuals," officials wrote at the time.

Around the same time, Maria caught the attention of the p
force in Windsor, the Canadian town right across the river from
troit and once a prime source of liquor smuggled into the Ur
States during Prohibition. The Windsor police had caught wind
newspaper ad for Maria in which she claimed "to know the secre
a mysterious 'luck attracting force' known as the Egrigor of Fri
the 13th." "Police investigation has revealed that 'Maria Duval' is
tually a 'front' used by a telemarketing firm based in the state of N
York," the Windsor police said in a scam warning at the time. "I
questionable whether 'Maria Duval' actually exists." In 2015, t
agency told us that it had been unable to find the person or peop
responsible, so no charges were ever filed.

Across the globe, Australian officials launched their own effor
to stop the scam in 2007, after discovering that victims had lost mor
than $10 million US dollars. Their investigation found that the mone
being sent in by Australian recipients was being rerouted to a com
pany in Singapore. This company was run by a man named Tony
(presumably the same Tony we had seen discussed on message
boards), who told investigators that the psychic was his client and
that she was in France or Argentina. When Australian reporters
confronted Tony in Singapore, accusing him of fabricating the psychic's existence, he claimed he would arrange for the reporters to
meet her in South America, but the meeting never occurred.

The mystery of Maria even reached the eight-thousand-person
town of Wolfurt, nestled in Austria's Rhine Valley. We emailed the

Could investigators be right? Could the woman at the center of this decades-long scam not even exist?

• • •

On a mission to test our suspicion that Maria Duval was nothing more than a lucrative work of fiction, we turned to the one group of people we thought might know best. If such a world-renowned clair-voyant truly existed, other self-proclaimed psychics would surely know her. Clearly we didn't have any on speed dial, so we started digging around online to find well-known psychics from around the world and blasted out an email with questions about Maria Duval, with no idea what would come of it.

Within a matter of hours, our first response came from a second-generation psychic whose earliest memories, we'd learn, were of playdates with the spirits of her deceased relatives. She none-theless had something to say about Maria. "I am sure that when you mention the name you don't get a very positive reaction from the psychic medium community—that is, those of us who do the work for the benefit of others and not for monetary gain," she wrote. "I do not know where she is any longer. She is alive. I do not, however, want my name associated with her in any way, shape or form. I'm sure you understand."

Responses continued to fly in. Several psychics said they hadn't heard of Maria at all and definitely didn't know her personally.

"I do not know her and I'm glad," wrote an Illinois psychic who makes regular talk radio appearances (according to her website). "There are so many fraudsters out there, and I feel I'm having to col-lectively work to establish credibility."

She said she was very skeptical that Maria was a real psychic like herself: "I tend to think she is a scammer. People who take advantage of people who are desperate are truly dark hearted, dangerous, and often deadly. I've steered many away from being scammed out of thousands."

How did these psychics come up with this stuff? Was this woman really suggesting Maria was a dangerous criminal? It wasn't an ordinary request, but we hadn't been expecting the responses to be quite so weird.

An hour later, emails were still pouring in—like this one, from a medium who claims to be able to connect people with deceased family and friends, as well as spirit guides and guardian angels: "Unfortunately I have met several folks pretending to be [Maria]," she wrote. "The last I did hear she had passed. Let me see what I can come up with."

And amid a string of duds came an email containing what appeared to be a full-on psychic reading—despite the fact that the psychic had never met her.

> I have never heard of Maria Duval but yes I believe she's alive. She's using another name possibly and she may be receiving treatment for illness related to smoking. That's all I can give you. I pick up nothing about this woman, not even psychic abilities. Be careful with this person. This is not her real name.

The psychic later wrote back with another tip:

> Btw do you think she's in Canada? I keep seeing the Canadian flag.

After another doozy about "universal energy" and "crown chakra" and one from someone claiming to be able to speak telepathically with animals, we didn't know how much more we could handle. But they kept coming. The founder of the American, Canadian & UK Associations of Psychics & Healers then chimed in, saying that she hadn't heard of Maria and that Maria definitely hadn't ever been a member of the organization. This seemed to be more proof she couldn't possibly exist. Wouldn't a psychic who gave consultations to international celebrities and politicians, as Maria's letters claimed, at least be known by this major psychic association?

There were more dead ends, like the messages from a self-proclaimed Reiki master, an "intuitive relationship analyst" from Australia, a professional tarot card reader, and a Canadian energy healer. Later that night, a New Mexico psychic told us she had been struck by a vision.

> I do Missing Persons work and as a Psychic myself, her eyes read "Help Me." Look at the people who she sold her work to. I feel that they may have scammed her herself, she may be caught in something that she cannot get out of. I feel that she went into hiding because of what she is caught in. This is the most likely reason that you cannot find her. I read her energy as "dead," but I believe that this is fear of what she is dealing with.

There were even more messages the next morning, including one from an animal communicator who had emailed us the previous day. The message was suspiciously similar to the reading that came the night before from the New Mexico psychic.

> Did a quick read on Maria Duval last night.
> Yes she is real.
> Yes she is alive.
> She is retired and not doing readings professionally for the public.

A scam company co-opted her likeness and reputation and ripped people off for money. Primary focus group being seniors and those with lower educational standards. She felt the only way to "fight" this unauthorized use of her name and likeness was to retire from publicity.

Heartbreaking really. So offensive.

The emails slowed to a trickle after that, and we were still unsure about whether Maria was real. All the colorful readings and predictions were amusing. We'd learn later, however, that some were eerily close to the truth.

. . .

While some of the psychics were adamant that Maria was real, their confidence seemed to be based on nothing more than their supposed psychic senses and visions. None of them had actually *met* her. Then, a few days before Halloween, a message came from the South of France, from a psychic named Véronique. There was just one problem: it was written in French. And as far as French went, neither of us could do much more than read a wine list.

The email arrived in the middle of the night, so we didn't see the message until the next morning. Preparing for our commutes into the office, we tried to decipher any words that we could. It soon became clear that Véronique was saying something important, something about meeting Maria. Eager to find out what the contents of this email held, we turned to Google Translate, which spit out the following:

Hello Blake,

Personally I have not seen since 1994, I know she did return on Callas in 2008 and later I heard from Customers that she had had problems with justice. Now I'll try to have more accurate information around me about Madame Maria Duval.

Wait a minute. Did something get lost in translation? Was she talking about the same woman? Could this psychic actually have met Maria Duval? The same Maria Duval from the letters? A few hours later, off the New York City subway and in the newsroom together at our adjacent desks, we reread the email again and again. Still in disbelief, we used Google Translate again to craft a message to send back, asking for more details of this personal encounter with Maria.

We waited anxiously, spending the time looking at Véronique's website hoping to gain a better sense of who we were dealing with. The homepage featured a bright purple background. There was a giant purple amethyst at the top, and a note in French explaining Véronique's uncanny psychic abilities: "My family gift was revealed in my childhood. In some places I felt strange, invisible sensations, I saw deceased. Faced with the people I perceived their intentions, images of the future."

She soon responded, and a colleague in our newsroom provided us with a rough translation:

> Yes I have already met Maria Duval in 1994 in a meeting at her office in Callas (France) for a consultation. I have nothing to say again about her work that day, [it was] a serious meeting. Following it, I never saw her again.
>
> If I have any more info, I'll let you know.
>
> Cordially,
>
> Véronique

We couldn't believe it.

We had found someone who claimed to have met this woman, albeit decades ago. True to form, as journalists, we were skeptical. All the evidence so far backed up our initial suspicion that a real Maria Duval was unlikely to be out there. Yet here was this woman claiming there actually was a psychic in the South of France with this very name.

Véronique fondly remembered her reading from Maria, though she didn't mention the letters going out around the world. Even if she was right about Maria's existence, we still needed to determine whether the Maria she'd allegedly met in France had anything to do with the letters—and if so, how she'd gotten wrapped up in all of this.

We shifted our focus to the paper trail, looking for any evidence to tie the Maria Duval from Véronique's consultation in Callas, France, to the letters. Our first hope was to locate birth, citizenship, or even death records from Italy, where both Wikipedia and the Maria Duval letters claimed she had been born. But the country's strict privacy rules meant that much of this information would be off limits. A similar search for citizenship or death records in France was also fruitless. So instead, we began digging up websites, government documents, articles, and other information on Maria and the letters that used her name over and over again.

The trail started more than thirty years ago, in 1985, as Ronald Reagan was sworn in for his second term as president, the Cold War dragged on, and the twenty-one-year-old Whitney Houston released her first album. The two of us hadn't even been born yet. This was when Maria (or someone pretending to be her) was granted a French trademark for the commercial use of the name "Maria Duval." Until now, we hadn't done much reporting on government trademarks, which help protect brand names and logos from copycats. We did know, however, that the main reason someone files for a trademark is to sell some kind of product or service.

Records from a French government website showed that the trademark was registered on September 13, 1985, through the trademark office in the seaside resort town of Nice. The documents described the nature of the business using a mixture of health and astrological terms that even to French novices like us were pretty easy to understand:

Produits pharmaceutiques, vétérinaires et hygiéniques, substances diététiques à usage médical, aliments pour bébés, emplâtres, matériel pour pansements, matières pour plomber les dents et pour empreintes dentaires, désinfectants, produits pour la destruction des animaux nuisibles, fongicides, herbicides. Vêtements, chaussures, chapellerie. Astrologie, parapsychologie, radiésthésie, cartomancie, voyance, futurologie.

Next to Maria's name, in the middle of the trademark document, was a French address: L'Estagnol, Les 4 Chemins, 83830 Callas, FR.

Callas. This was the same tiny town where Wikipedia had told us we would find her. It was where Véronique told us she had met Maria for a reading. The letters even referenced Callas, saying Maria was the leader of the Institute for Parapsychological Research there.

A number of other trademarks for "Maria Duval" had been issued across the globe in the decades following this first trademark. Maria was listed as the applicant on many of them, and a number also listed attorneys who represented her. We contacted all of these lawyers to see if they could help us get in touch with Maria. None of them claimed to have met her in person, nor had they spoken to her.

One New York–based, Harvard-educated attorney who represented Maria in 1995 for her first trademark in the United States, for example, said that while he had represented someone by that name, he "never had direct contact with that person" and dealt only with an overseas attorney by airmail. His last communication with this attorney, who he said was a woman named Andrea Egger, was in 2003. "I don't know whether anyone involved is alive now or how to find them, if alive."

This all seemed very suspicious. A trademark filed solely via airmail? His email did little to confirm whether Maria Duval existed and whether she really had been the person applying for a trademark. But it did introduce us for the first time to Andrea Egger, whose name would eventually become almost as familiar to us as Maria's. We would later determine he was actually a male (not a female) attorney from Switzerland. Months down the road, we would end up in a dark, winding hallway outside his door. But that comes later.

We also had a puzzling exchange with a different attorney from a firm that represented Maria on a Canadian trademark just a few years after the US one. "It does not appear that we have had any additional contact with Maria Duval since 1997," the attorney wrote.

Not satisfied with this one-line response, we quickly responded. "Does this mean that your agency did have direct contact with Maria Duval in 1997? We're trying to figure out if she was actually involved in the trademark application or if it was someone else. If so, do you know if anyone met her in person?"

But again, all we got back was a cryptic reply. "I'm sorry, I don't have any additional information that I can pass along to you on this matter." This left us wondering whether this attorney too had communicated only with this Andrea Egger character and not Maria.

It was an attorney from Finland, whose firm had represented Maria on a 1996 trademark, who was the most candid of the bunch:

Normally our firm cannot give any information about our clients, but given the rather historical aspect of your investigation I take the liberty of telling you that we did not have any contact with Maria Duval after filing a trademark for her in 1996. A quick investigation on Google reveals that she has visited Finland in year 2000 and there were some media reports about her visit. These things were probably connected.

Unfortunately there is not much more I can tell you, I wish you good luck in tracking her down!

Again, we asked if this meant he had been in direct contact with Maria while filing the trademark. And again the answer was no.

Despite their dry legalese, we were convinced that these attorneys held the key to figuring out whether the woman in Callas was behind the letters. The trademark documents themselves, on which her name was clearly listed as the applicant, suggested she was. Since none of these attorneys seemed to have ever met or spoken to her, it seemed entirely possible that someone else pretending to be Maria could have easily orchestrated all these filings.

But then we found a 2006 trademark document that featured a signature that was allegedly from Maria—and it looked a lot like the signature on all the scam letters. In this document, filed with the US Patent and Trademark Office, Maria pledged that she was a "living individual" and consented to the registration of a trademark for her name. Of course, someone could have been brazen enough to forge this signature despite the grave legal consequences for doing so. Otherwise, it appeared that Maria Duval really had been involved with filing these trademarks. As far as we could tell, Maria or someone pretending to be her was filing for trademarks so that her name could be used to solicit money, just as the letters had done for decades.

There was also a detail in the email from the Finnish attorney that made Maria's involvement seem more possible. He wrote that a real woman claiming to be Maria Duval made a public appearance in Finland not long after the trademark was filed. Could this appearance have been used to lure in potential victims?

· · ·

Tabloids and other news reports about Maria showed her traveling the world making in-person media appearances.

An online video appeared to document her visit to Finland. The woman in the video looked middle aged and had the same short blond hair as the younger woman pictured in the letters. At one point, she swung around some sort of pendulum, and another shot showed her looking at tarot cards. We couldn't understand what was being said in the video, but it was pretty clear that she was being touted in Finland as a true psychic.

Right around the time she allegedly visited Finland, she had also traveled to Australia. Maria, or whoever it was claiming to be her, had been interviewed by a radio host named Maria Zijlstra at the government-funded Australian Broadcasting Corporation. In her head shot online, Maria Zijlstra is pictured as a middle-aged woman in narrow, red-rimmed glasses with a long braid going from her forehead down past her shoulders. And her bio didn't read like that of a typical journalist: "As a preschooler, Maria Zijlstra smashed the family radio by inadvertently pulling it off the top of a slopey-shouldered refrigerator, for which she is still trying to make amends."

After weeks emailing back and forth with officials at the Australian radio station, we received the audio file of the entire fifteen-minute interview, which was taped in 1999 but not aired until January 2000 (right after the fears of a Y2K apocalypse had subsided). Eager to hear how the interview unfolded, we plugged in our headphones and listened from our computers, pausing every few seconds in order to transcribe each sentence.

From the interview, you would never know the controversy that was already swirling around Maria and the letters bearing her name. In fact, the letters were raging in Australia and New Zealand at the very same time the interview was conducted. The interview was also, suspiciously enough, conducted remotely—meaning that the host was not in the same room as Maria or her interpreter. The woman claiming to be Maria was given the opportunity to spend the entire time boasting about her extrasensory abilities.

The host began the interview by lavishing her with a fawning introduction.

Her curriculum vitae presents her as having twenty-three years of accurate and verifiable political and economic predictions under her belt, including that Jacques Chirac would become the president of France. . . . Cooperating with doctors and police, she has located nineteen missing persons so far, and she has had thousands of appearances in the media, mainly providing horoscopes and mainly in Europe, but her territory of influence is growing to include Australia, since last year anyway. I met Maria Duval then on her visit here to Australia, catching her actually just before she left the country and then only by studio hookup while she was in Sydney. . . .

Now she used an interpreter, I hasten to tell you, since she claims her English isn't good enough, but despite that I found her powers of communication extremely impressive—or maybe I'm a sucker. By the way, she began our conversation by asking me when I was born, complimenting me on my star sign.

Maria (the psychic) started by talking about how intrigued she had always been with Australia, and went on to discuss her work with the supposed Callas Institute for Parapsychological Research and whether particular nationalities were more open to psychics than others. Then we got to the good part, where Maria mentioned some sort of "commercial structure" and seemed to at least hint that she could be involved with the letters or the company sending them out.

The gifts that I received at birth which I've developed give me a much more human dimension. What does that mean to have that human dimension if it isn't to be able to help large numbers of people, people who meet us or who write to us? We have a service established so we respond to these people and we give them help. Not only psychic but also material help. Naturally through my work we've established a commercial structure, that's normal. But through my skills, our aim is to help as many people as possible. Because at the moment, people, at least those who live in very sophisticated civilizations, have no point of grounding. Religions are disappearing. The family structure is no longer what it was. So most people need to refer to and to tell their troubles to somebody, and I hope that I am fulfilling that role.

What we considered to be a scam Maria made sound like a noble venture. Instead of pressing her on this, the host only fed her ego:

It sounds to some degree the way you've described it as if you are kind of a social worker, but then on a mass scale. Is that a fair kind of way of summing it up?

Yes, Maria responded.

It was the host's complete lack of skepticism that caught our attention. Hearing her glorify Maria Duval as a social worker made our blood boil. The interview got even more outrageous from there, with Maria talking about how she predicted the new prime minister of Sweden after being shown only a photo and how "the greatest scientists" placed electrodes on her brain in a failed attempt to find the source of her powers. The segment ended with her making outlandish predictions about the end of civilization as we know it.

We're going to be living in space. For the moment, there are actually no references in our civilization for that. So the planet Mars will soon be explored. If there's evidence of water there—and where there's water there is the possibility of life. And if humans manage planet earth so badly, the future history will be written in space. With stations in space of three thousand, five hundred people. There will be more and more of those. And earth in about one hundred years' time will explode because of poor management of the humans.

Apparently Maria Duval was a doomsayer. We didn't know how this story could possibly get any stranger.

. . .

It was 2007 when Belgian journalist Jan Vanlangendonck and his colleagues arranged a sit-down interview with Maria at a Paris hotel. After suffering through the glowing Australian interview, we were happy to find another journalist who shared many of the same questions about Maria that we had.

In a series of radio reports that aired before the meeting, Jan took a much more skeptical approach than the Australian radio host, documenting the Maria Duval letters as a heartless scam. He said that Maria's "secretary," Jacques Mailland, had told him that Maria had agreed to meet him in order to defend herself against the negative way he had portrayed her in his reports.

We watched the interview on YouTube. It was originally shown on a Belgian television program called *Koppen*. We immediately recognized the elderly French-speaking woman with dyed blond hair and unnaturally plump lips. She wore a silky royal blue blouse and flashy black leather pants. Her voice sounded a lot like the one from the Australian radio interview from nearly a decade earlier. We both decided that the woman from the video and the woman in the grainy photo on the letters that showed a much younger glamorous blond could indeed be the same woman, especially if in recent years she had gotten some major plastic surgery.

In the interview Maria likened herself to an angel and berated journalists for attacking her with negative articles. When asked about the letters in her name, she admitted that she didn't sign each letter but still defended the operation, saying in French that the majority of her clients were happy, while those who were unsatisfied were offered refunds.

I have people that I've trained. I cannot write day and night. . . .
I take the responsibility. I'm certain that my people are well
trained. They may sign for me. I don't understand why you
would make it into a controversy when people are free to reply,
when they receive a prepaid stamped envelope on which they
can indicate if they do not want to receive mail from Maria
Duval, when if they are not satisfied after six months, they can
be reimbursed. What more could you want? . . . In conclusion,
I'm very pleased with myself. I've been working for fifty years,
and for fifty years, the majority of the testimonials we get are
satisfied. So poor Maria Duval works so hard on something she
loves, helping other people. I don't see why all the negative ar-
ticles [have been written]. . . . I've dedicated my life to helping
others.

If the letters were really someone else's creation, this interview
would have been Maria's chance to distance herself from the scam.
Instead she did the opposite. She vehemently defended the letters
sent in her name, seeming oblivious to the pain she had caused.

We later spoke with Jan, who still remembered Maria vividly. He
described her in an email as "mad(!), but a cunning lady, sly as a fox.

"She never stepped out of her character," he wrote.

At this point, we were becoming human Ping-Pong balls. In
only a matter of weeks, our theories had bounced all over the place.
We went from thinking Maria was a psychic villain to thinking she
was nothing more than a stock image. Then we started to believe
that Maria might be a real person, a real person who claimed to be a
psychic. What we needed to confirm was her involvement with the
letters.

The Psychic Sidekick

W E WERE NOW convinced that Maria Duval was real and that there had to be someone out there who could help us find her.

Her sidekick Patrick Guerin, the man whose letters and corny DVD initially sparked our interest in this investigation, might be the right person to start with, we figured. Maria's letters often introduced Patrick as her friend and esteemed colleague. It was likely that whoever had turned Patrick into a mail-order psychic may have been behind Maria's fame too.

Patrick's letters hadn't garnered nearly the attention—or the complaints—that Maria's had. Patrick, it seems, was used as a tool to suck even more money out of victims who were already obsessed with Maria.

I wouldn't normally take a telephone call while I'm doing this kind of meticulous work since it can be very distracting and I need to stay totally concentrated. But this time I had a strange feeling that this call was different. More importantly, I had a feeling that it was directly linked to the work I was doing for you. And I wasn't wrong!

When I picked up the handset, I recognized the warm, gentle voice of my friend, the renowned psychic, Patrick Guerin.

This seer has a worldwide reputation. He also has the rare and special power to make people <u>win, win and WIN AGAIN at the lottery</u> and other games of "chance", very often really large amounts of money!

In this letter, Maria goes on to explain in great detail how she and Patrick had the same fantastic vision about the very person reading the letter. She writes how the two of them spent days locked in a room, working together "around the clock to perfect a brilliant, unique and very dynamic and personalized help plan."

Can you imagine the situation? Two acclaimed and respected psychics having the <u>same visions</u> about you <u>at the same time</u>! And in those visions, we both saw you winning a <u>large</u> sum of money on the lottery very soon and solving all those urgent problems that have been casting a shadow over your life until now! In such circumstances, how could everything we've seen for you not come true! <u>Two</u> psychics of international renown can't be wrong!

Among the psychic notes Maria claims she and Patrick took:

Powerball!
SEVERAL WINNINGS!!!
Rebirth!

Like Maria, Patrick also claimed to be French. He had a very active Facebook page, which featured a circle of colorful tarot cards as its cover photo, placed above a profile photo of the same serious-looking man with wavy brown hair from the letter in our pile of junk mail.

His business website also popped up, which advertised more than a dozen books he had written, along with his consultations. On Google Street View the address for these consultations brought us to a nine-story apartment building with a bookstore on its ground floor and a *crêperie* next door. Maybe Patrick lived in the building or used the bookstore for consultations.

Our best shot to speak with Patrick would be to secure a meeting with him, so we decided to pose as interested customers, planning to later identify ourselves as journalists if he agreed to a meeting. Patrick's email address was right on his website, so we sent him this carefully crafted message:

Dear Patrick,

I am from the United States and saw one of your letters. I would like to come to Paris for a psychic reading. How do I schedule this?

Two days later, he sent us a response in French: "Do you speak French? In that case I would welcome you."

Excited to hear back from him, we responded again to say that we could bring a French-speaking friend, asked him how to schedule a meeting, and where his office was located.

To this, there was no response. We tried calling the phone number from his website, which resulted in a voice mail advertising his psychic services, and emailed him again. For a brief moment, we had a glimmer of hope that we would be jetting to Paris to meet this rosy-cheeked clairvoyant face-to-face, after which we imagined him spilling all of Maria's dirty secrets. Such a trip, however, was clearly not in the cards. We never received more from him than that single email.

The Sightings

WITHOUT PATRICK, WE returned to the growing list of Maria's media appearances.

One of the last recorded sightings of her was a high-profile appearance in Russia in 2008, which had been documented extensively in videos online and photos posted on Flickr by a user named "Maria Duval" (a user who, upon further research, appeared to have uploaded these photos and nothing else). Maria had even held a press conference at the Central House of Journalists in Moscow, complete with an official press release and fancy programs that announced her visit.

Maria Duval, the famous French medium and clairvoyant, holds an open meeting in Moscow devoted to forecast the future of the Russian society. Among the announced topics of the meeting— the astrological forecast for the next few years, the results of the forthcoming elections in the United States, the resolution of the Russian-Georgian conflict, the development of nanotechnology.

The press release, which was written in Russian, went on to detail an elaborate history of Maria in a manner very similar to the story told in so many of the letters and detailed in the Australian radio interview, including that she lived "in seclusion in her beloved Provence" and had written countless books. It also included some of her most repeated claims to fame: that she was the only psychic to have been granted a visit with the pope and that she had once found Brigitte Bardot's dog. From its tone, you would think it was heralding the arrival of a queen.

Maria was caught on camera as she entered the black wrought iron gates of the building wearing oversized sunglasses, a short black skirt and jacket, black heels, and a bright red scarf. The footage showed that the press conference was attended by a room full of people, including many holding video cameras and notepads, and close-up camera shots showed Maria's chunky, braided metallic necklace, cleavage-revealing top, star-shaped earrings, and heavily applied icy eye shadow. Behind her hung a regal banner bearing a large "D," presumably for "Duval."

It was during this visit that Maria predicted that "the next president of the United States will be black," conveniently making the call just a few weeks before the election took place, at a time when Barack Obama was leading in the polls. And the Russian media, which broadcast the prediction, seemed to be far more impressed than we were. Some of her other predictions included that the US dollar would collapse and that the next generation would be more adept at using computers (imagine that!).

We had already seen evidence that Maria Duval's letters had been going out in Russia in recent years. Could this trip have been some kind of a launch party?

Curiously, only a few months after all the fanfare of that Russian visit, her global media tour seemed to have come to a halt, suggesting that Maria had entered into a retirement of sorts. In December 2008, a French newspaper celebrated her return to the small town of Callas, the same town listed on all those trademark applications. "Maria Duval: the return that nobody had predicted," the headline read in French.

Maria Duval, the return! A great adventurer in the face of the eternal, the lady left Callas after 12 years. Not to retire, in fact, the opposite—to travel the world and immerse herself in different spiritualities while sharing her gifts with the world.

She must have missed the Var province, since she returned to her Callas home, where she said she wants to put herself at the service of individuals and politicians who would like to know parts of their future.

The text was accompanied by a photo of the same elderly blond woman wearing the same silver star earrings and the same plumped lips, staring stoically into the distance from behind the leaves of a tree. Most intriguing, the article said that back in Callas, Maria would continue to sell books and amulets through the mail. It was unclear to us how the journalist had sourced the information about Maria, and whether or not the reporter actually had spoken with her.

The article detailed many of Maria's travels we had already discovered through our research: Australia, where she reportedly spent time with Aborigines. And Russia, where it said 700,000 apple trees had been planted in her name. It also mentioned two trips that were new to us: a visit to India, where she reportedly discovered yoga and stayed in an ashram, and South America, where it said she was initiated into shamanism, a tradition centered on healing and spirituality.

She then finally came home.

For how long will our ambitious globe-trotter keep her suitcases down in Callas? No one can predict, but she puts forward: "I am available for other adventures!"

• • •

Even after her reported retirement in 2008, the letters bearing Maria's name and image continued to relentlessly arrive in victims' mailboxes. US investigators later found that huge batches of tens of thousands of letters had been going out in the United States and Canada as recently as 2014, while reports detailed the recent existence of letters in many other countries.

One 2014 Russian news article, for example, reported that retirees stormed the offices of a company in Moscow where they believed they could claim the winnings they had been promised in Maria Duval's letters. Her letters even fooled a doctor in a remote part of Kazakhstan, according to another article.

Since the French newspaper article said Maria would still be selling psychic products, we wondered if she could be pulling the strings of this operation from her home in Callas. Or maybe she hadn't really retired as the article had claimed.

In late 2009, a series of videos began popping up on YouTube. Six clips with English subtitles showed the same elderly woman from the Russian press conference. They were all published on the same day, October 27, and they were posted again the next day, this time with subtitles in various Asian languages. Each of the videos was posted by a YouTube user named "gd2use."

After we watched the videos, we determined that the uploader was either a devoted follower or someone somehow connected to the letters, or both. Before this six-part series, gd2use had also uploaded a number of homemade videos featuring newspaper clips and Maria's on-camera interviews from various countries.

And then there was a three-part series with English subtitles. One of these crude videos included nothing more than poorly cropped grainy images and clip art and looked like something an elementary school student would have put together in the 1990s. The video was narrated dramatically by a woman speaking a language we couldn't immediately pinpoint, and within the subtitles were some interesting claims about the psychic.

> *The first time she became aware of her supernatural gifts was when she was given a difficult assignment at school. She closed her eyes and saw the solution in front of her. But she had not explain how she had come by her solution, and was punished for it instead of appreciated. Also at school, she noticed another of her talents when she cured a teacher of a persistent cold. It became clear to her then that she had healing powers at her disposal.*

The letters mostly talked about her seeing better health in people's futures; this was the first time we had heard anything about Maria being a healer.

One video in the series even included images of handwritten notes in different languages, which it claimed had been sent directly to Maria by her satisfied customers. One of these testimonials was particularly odd, seeming to suggest that Maria was responsible for the untimely death of someone's boss, leading to a miraculous promotion.

> *Dear Maria Duval,*
>
> *Everything you have done for me is great. I was offered a job I enjoyed very much, but when I had worked there for a few weeks, the manager suddenly passed away, and then, miracles, they asked me if I felt up to the challenge, we still have to get used to so much prosperity, but now we are beginning to believe in it, that all the negative waves around us have disappeared thanks to your help.*

Apparently, she could even tell just by looking at someone how much longer he or she would live.

> *When she walks in the street she could see faces of passersby change into the faces of old people. Sometimes she sees a face that hardly changes, and she knows this person won't live long.*

Who was this anonymous person, calling him- or herself gd2use, spending all this time uploading these videos and promoting Maria? Especially after she had allegedly retired? Since YouTube protects the privacy of its users, we attempted our own detective work. Searching the obscure username online brought up nothing else but the videos, so the only thing left to do was watch all twenty-nine videos gd2use had uploaded to see if there were any clues.

The very first video, in early 2007, was simply titled "Maria Duval is real." It featured a compilation of Maria Duval clips and almost looked like a recording of someone's computer screen.

There was only one that wasn't about the psychic. Titled "Jumping Dog," this clip had 168 views (partly because we watched it so many times), a small number compared with the thousands of views the Maria Duval videos had received. In the clip you see a man's blue jeans and hear a woman's voice saying "Jump" over and over in heavily accented English as a small Dachshund-like brown dog jumps up and down in front of the man's legs. At the end of the seven-second video, another small white dog partially enters the frame.

We were hoping this video could give us some clues about gd2use's mysterious identity. It didn't. We returned to the six videos the user posted on the same day. The first was "Maria Duval on mail clairvoyance." Then came "Maria Duval on her Consultation," "Maria Duval—How she uses pendulum to locate missing people," "Maria Duval—Interesting encounters in her psychic works," "Maria Duval—Her magical talisman," and finally, "Maria Duval—Her natural gift."

It appeared that all these videos had been part of the same film shoot, as Maria was dressed in the same outfit for each and was seated at the same desk, with a wooden statue resembling the Virgin Mary looking over her shoulder. These videos were of much higher quality than the crude compilations of media interviews that gd2use had also posted. Whoever shot them, it seems, had been sitting in the same room with Maria.

In the videos, Maria is wearing a black V-neck sweater, a simple diamond necklace, and pale pink lipstick on the same plumped lips we'd seen in other interviews. We even spotted the same silver star earrings in her ears. In them, much of the time she's in front of the camera, talking about how she cultivated her special gift, saying it all started when she was a young girl.

> When I was a child I had this gift, but I thought it was something that everybody had. So I wasn't surprised when I had clairvoyant flashes. It was only after several years that I finally understood that I was different, because I realized I wasn't like other people. And they made me see there was something in me that was more highly developed than it is in others. So I started to have these visions and little by little I became less worried about having these visions that actually used to frighten me when I was young.

Maria says she gradually learned to accept—and even embrace—this gift. And as a result, she explains that she has used her powers to succeed in every job she had over the years. She says she scouted talented artists for two Avenue Matignon art galleries in Paris, helped a large bank choose senior executives by conducting astrological tests, and assisted "heads of industry" in starting ventures like atomic power stations.

She also talks about performing exorcisms, including one of a young woman that left Maria with third-degree burns on her knees. And she says she has long performed individual psychic consultations, even though they sometimes make her feel uncomfortable. In one example, she tells the story of a woman who arrived at her office in disguise and tried to get Maria to tell her whether her dead husband cheated on her with any of the women on a list of names.

Her true success, Maria says, didn't come until the media launched her, which she claims was completely against her will.

I found it so embarrassing to charge money, that for a whole year I saw around thirty people a day and never asked for a single penny, because it seemed to me that this ability I had was a gift and I didn't want to exploit it. It was only later of course that I became professional. Events overtook me.

Events overtook her? For someone who was embarrassed to charge for her services, the letters in her name sure raked in a lot of money.

Some of the other media interviews we had seen were more cryptic about her involvement with the letters. They vaguely mentioned a "commercial structure" and were clearly meant to convince people that she was real, that she was the one giving guidance through the mail. We even found the entire video uploaded by gd2use that was devoted to her so-called talismans, the cheap trinkets that were sent to people once they paid up.

People very often ask me how I can work by correspondence, and time and time again, people say to me, Listen, there's no way you can know. No way you can respond to a very specific problem of a person you don't know who sends you a letter. So how? It's very simple, it's the same as when someone comes to see me at my office. First of all, I look at your handwriting, then I take your date of birth—and don't doubt that the major contours of life are written with the date of birth. There's a knack I have. I can see through what people say, read between the lines, if you like. I draw on my intuition, and I very often find the solution to problems, even though people aren't always truthful in their letters. So I've developed a knack, I've become quite expert. . . . I work with a team of collaborators, men and women in whom I have absolute faith who've been working with me for more than ten years, and who are trained, and we make a good team. You can rest assured that I look at the great majority of your letters.

After seeing this, it was undeniable: we still had no idea how much money this woman actually received from the letters, but she was clearly involved. We quickly ran through all the pieces of the puzzle we had gathered so far:

The French psychic Véronique told us that back in the 1990s she had had a consultation in Callas with a psychic named Maria Duval. For decades, a blond woman had traveled the globe touting her powers, and sometimes even defending the letters. During this same time, a woman with this name was filing trademarks for some sort of business venture. Now here was the very same woman from the media appearances staring at us through the camera, saying she could establish psychic contact by mail. In the video, she promises that she reads almost all the letters sent to her—the very same letters investigators later found discarded in a Long Island Dumpster. Many of the stories she told in these videos also matched, almost word for word, what we'd read in the letters and seen on versions of her old US websites.

Through all of this, a constant became clear: It was the same Maria.

The Dentist's Wife

ACROSS ALL THE letters, interviews, and websites we pored over, one key manifestation of Maria's power was repeatedly touted: her uncanny ability to locate the missing.

In the videos, she says her efforts have included finding missing children, though she stopped doing so after finding it too painful to inform parents that their beloved child was "dead or gone forever." And she doesn't stop at humans, having used her powers to locate missing animals as well. "I successfully located a dog belonging to Brigitte Bardot," she says in one video. "I've found not less famous cats, and I even found a donkey that had got lost. You see, there are no limits on what you can find."

One of the most repeated stories of Maria's telepathic abilities was so fantastical that it was hard to take even remotely seriously. The story, detailed on the archived version of her website, was supposedly recounted by an unidentified writer who described himself as a skeptic of Maria and her powers. This person claimed to have met Maria after she had become the heroine of a "bizarre drama" involving a dentist and his wife, though it was unclear when exactly this all occurred. "I had in fact come to ask her about her powers and to try and understand how someone in this day and age can call themselves a clairvoyant," the individual stated.

The story sounded like something out of a movie: A young dentist's wife disappears in the ritzy French resort town of Saint-Tropez. She is last seen driving off in her car on a weekday afternoon. The next morning, her abandoned car is found by hikers on a treacherous hillside pass with no clues as to where she has gone. Police from multiple seaside towns send out search parties, calling on members of the local fire brigade and even dispatching Drole IV—"the best police dog in the region"—to help with the hunt. Two helicopter teams search from sunrise to sunset, but the woman's whereabouts remain a mystery. By Friday, all hope is lost.

That's when Maria steps in.

Using only a map of the area and the woman's photo and birthdate, Maria works her magic. First, she places the photo of the dentist's wife on top of the unfolded map. She then holds her pendulum, described in the story as a "hanging lamp," over the map and photo. The lamp starts to move back and forth slowly. Then suddenly it begins to swing in smaller and smaller circles, eventually zeroing in on a specific point that is not far from one of the oldest villages in the South of France.

The police are skeptical. The dentist, desperate and willing to try anything, pays a helicopter pilot to take him to where Maria is adamant the woman will be found.

And there she is.

She lay under fir trees wounded and unconscious. She had lay there for three days and nights without anything to eat or drink and without being able to move. She hadn't even been able to wave to the helicopters that had flown over her. If Maria hadn't done anything the young woman would have died of starvation and distress. . . . Maria could not have known, by any means, where the poor woman had fallen. In other words: she had found the woman with her hanging lamp—and with that alone.

Earlier, we had dismissed this report as just another piece of fantasy, until we suddenly heard Maria herself talking about a very similar story in one of the many YouTube videos posted by the mysterious gd2use. In it, Maria recounts how, after her powers were questioned, she ultimately used a map to locate a missing person, flying by helicopter to find the missing person barely alive.

But then came an important realization. As we replayed the video, it became clear that even though it seemed that Maria could be talking about the same saga that had been detailed by the skeptic, her version had one big inconsistency: In Maria's video, the missing person was a male pilot whose plane had crashed. The missing person from the story on the website was a dentist's wife.

It was an entirely different missing person.

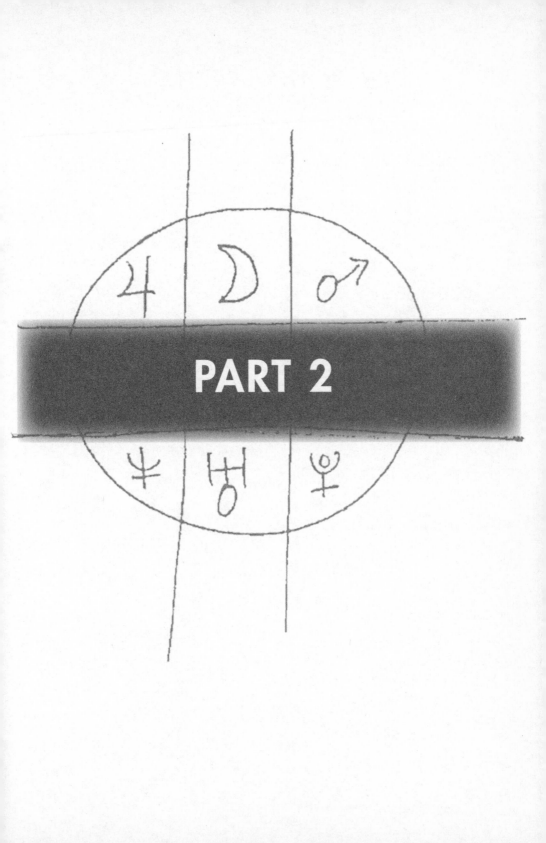

PART 2

The Investigators

A N INTRIGUING AND little-known branch of law enforcement holed up in a row of Washington, DC, offices was determined to stop the Maria Duval letters once and for all. For the investigators of the United States Postal Inspection Service (USPIS), this case of mail fraud was less about Maria Duval and more about the massive web of businesses behind the scam.

The USPIS, which falls under the jurisdiction of the US Postal Service, investigates crimes in which the perpetrator has used the mail in some way to carry out his or her illicit activities. Unlike the workers you see at the post office or delivering the mail, US postal inspectors carry guns, surveil and arrest criminals, execute search warrants, and use the power of subpoenas. More than a dozen investigators have been killed in the line of duty, and the agency even has its own forensic crime lab, where scientists test for drugs, analyze fingerprints, and conduct chemical examinations of potential explosives found in the mail.

Founded by Benjamin Franklin before the United States was even a country, the USPIS has a surprisingly colorful past—which we had never heard anything about before finding it detailed on the agency's website. In the early twentieth century, the agency was responsible for arresting fourteen suspected members of a secret criminal society known as the "Black Hand." This group, which had its own school where it trained assassins, was infamous in cities with large populations of Italian immigrants. The extortionists and blackmailers who made up the society were known to send terrifying, threatening letters through the mail, marked by a large hand drawn in black ink. The letters would warn immigrants that their families would be hurt, their children would be kidnapped, their houses would be burned down, and they would end up murdered if they didn't hand over a specific sum of money, often thousands of dollars. Postal inspectors were crucial to ending this extortion.

Not long after this triumph, the agency solved "the last known robbery" of a horse-drawn mail carriage; these robberies had been one of the country's earliest forms of mail crime. And then, in 1920, postal inspectors were tasked with putting an end to a much more sophisticated crime. This time, they attempted to unravel the pyramid investment fraud run by Charles Ponzi, the infamous conman who gave Ponzi schemes their name. Inspectors discovered that Ponzi had used his alluring charm to convince thirty thousand people to join a complicated foreign investment scheme. Yet it would turn out that Ponzi's supposed investment miracle was all a mirage. Instead of going to investors, much of the $10 million he brought in went to fund his own flashy lifestyle, complete with a gold-handled walking stick and piles of $10,000 bills he showed off to admirers, as he paid old investors with the money brought in by his newest victims. Ponzi was ultimately charged and convicted of mail fraud because he'd sent physical letters to victims encouraging them to reinvest in his scheme. The five-year prison sentence he received was just the beginning. Ponzi would go on to dupe people into investing in Florida swampland, and he later unsuccessfully tried to flee the United States disguised as a ship worker.

He then spent more time in prison before being deported to his native Italy, where he would steal from the state treasury. He eventually died broke and alone in a charity hospital in Brazil. His name, however, as the USPIS explains on its website, lives on in infamy as a label used to brand the present-day frauds of men like Bernie Madoff and Allen Stanford (the case our USPIS source, Clayton, had worked on and compared to the Maria Duval scam).

In the 1920s there was an international manhunt for three "train bandits" who killed four men and blew up a mail car as it exited a tunnel in southern Oregon. The DeAutremont brothers had been convinced that the train was transporting half a million dollars in gold, but in fact they found nothing of value inside. Using excessive amounts of dynamite, the brothers killed one person in the blast, and they shot three others as they fled the scene. Postal inspectors eventually apprehended the bandits after more than three years of intense searching.

This same agency, almost a hundred years later, now had its sights set on the Maria Duval letters, today's version of a heartless crime relying on the mail to prey on its victims.

It all started with a postal inspector named Thomas Ninan. An unassuming middle-aged man, Thomas had been with the agency since 2003 and had worked on countless wire and mail fraud cases over the years. At the time, he was part of a special mail fraud task force that worked in conjunction with the US Department of Justice.

One day in March 2014, Thomas was paging through bank records subpoenaed for a completely different investigation when he noticed something out of the ordinary. An alarming number of withdrawal requests were being denied for payments to one business in particular, with an intriguing name: Destiny Research Center.

Thomas didn't know it at the time, but Destiny Research Center was the company used to send letters from both Maria Duval and

Patrick Guerin. Registered in Hong Kong, Destiny Research Center was supposedly headed up by Martin Dettling, a Swiss man who the US government would later learn had opened the mailboxes we visited in Sparks. It was this company that would soon take over much of Thomas's days and nights, as he became wrapped up in the very same mystery we were now trying to solve.

. . .

The US government's investigation started much like ours.

"I performed a simple Google search for Destiny Research Center and was immediately struck by vast numbers of consumer complaints on websites and Internet bulletin boards, describing the fraud that had been committed by Destiny Research Center for many years," Thomas said in a court filing. "Based on my initial review of these consumer complaints and evidence gathered later in the investigation, it appears that many, if not most, consumers who receive solicitations are vulnerable victims, including the desperate, elderly, ill-educated, and infirm."

Using subpoena powers we wished we had, Thomas and his colleagues were then gradually able to zero in on the complicated business network behind the letters and uncover all the layers used to obscure the flow of money from its victims. With enough evidence of an illicit mail operation, the USPIS teamed up with prosecutors from the Department of Justice to take legal action against the people and businesses they believed were at the heart of the scheme. The accused included both American and Canadian companies directly involved with the distribution of the letters, though it was unclear if they were their true source. The government's lawsuit and related criminal investigation were already well under way when we started looking into the scam, but it took until mid-2016 for the government to secure a court order from a judge to permanently bar the letters from going out in the United States.

It turned out that the name Maria Duval wasn't new to the US government. Back in 2007, the USPIS filed a cease-and-desist order against her operation and a company called Zodiac Zone, which appeared to be nothing more than a name used when sending her letters. Instead of following the order, the people in charge of the mailings appear to have simply changed the company's name to Destiny Research Center and continued to send the letters out en masse.

The documents from the most recent government lawsuit provided us with crucial information about how these businesses had evaded US and Canadian authorities for so long. They were also some of the most fascinating court documents we had ever read, providing a step-by-step look at the twisted path the letters took before reaching each victim. It was a colorful story of deception not unlike the wild tales told about Charles Ponzi.

The US letters all started with a small Canadian firm named Infogest Direct Marketing. Officially known to the Canadian government by the generic name 9097-9394 Québec Inc., this company was located in downtown Montreal and had a small staff of no more than five employees. Thomas ultimately discovered that Infogest managed the Maria Duval mailings dating back to the 2000s. From 2006 to 2014, the company was behind at least fifty-six million Maria Duval and Patrick Guerin letters, mailing an average of seven million a year. (It was hard for the US government to separate the two psychics when counting all the letters, since many of them included the names of both individuals. We determined from our research that Patrick was just a sidekick who first appeared in the letters in recent years.)

In an attempt to avoid detection, Infogest sent the letters zigzagging around North America before they landed in victims' mailboxes. First, an unnamed company in Canada was hired by Infogest to print the letters, which the US government says were addressed to thousands of mainly elderly Americans whose names and addresses had been found on lists bought from data brokers. While these lists can be used by legitimate retailers, marketers, and charities, the information on them can end up in the hands of criminals, who use such lists to find the perfect victims for their schemes. For example, a senior who repeatedly sends money in response to charity solicitations may be passionate about a cause. But scammers see something entirely different; they see a sign that a person's memory might be failing. Maybe such a person is unable to remember how frequently she is donating her money. If this is the case, maybe she will respond to other, less charitable offers as well.

We also learned that advertisements placed in newspapers in the United States and around the world have solicited personal data. Some of these ads claimed to be offering Maria's services for free, while others didn't mention her name at all. Instead they asked readers to send in everything from their zodiac sign and time of birth to their marital status, all under the guise of a research study in which the participants were eligible to win large amounts of money. This personal information was then automatically incorporated into the letter, making the correspondence feel even more believable to its victim, who would be amazed that Maria somehow knew his or her birthday or hometown.

Government documents showed that after being printed and addressed, the letters were then shipped by truck across the Canadian border (by the same unnamed company that printed the letters) to Albany, New York, where they were mailed out in batches of as many as fifty thousand at a time.

Once the letters arrived and were opened, recipients were instructed to mail their payments, personal information, photos, and
locks of hair to Maria or Patrick, in the care of Destiny Research
Center at one of its US or Canadian addresses (including the one we
visited in Sparks). We suspected that Destiny Research Center was
nothing more than a shell company used as another layer to obscure
the operation. And, as we found in Sparks, the return addresses for
Destiny Research Center turned out to be just commercial mailboxes opened by the mysterious man from Switzerland, Martin
Dettling.

The path didn't end there. At these mailbox locations, employees
were instructed to bundle the mail from the scam's victims and send
it all to a completely different company located in Long Island, New
York. This mail ended up at an office suite in a boxy bank building in
an industrial park with a single tree out front and an American flag
hanging from a flagpole in the parking lot, just across the street from
a 1-800-Radiator, among other run-of-the-mill businesses. When we
looked up the building on Google Street View, we even saw a US
Postal Service truck parked out front. The company had a generic
name, Data Marketing Group Ltd., and it was run by a woman named
Keitha Rocco, who was once honored as Woman of the Year by a
local chapter of the American Cancer Society. In an archived version
of its website, the company said it helped marketing clients manage
databases full of customers, blast out promotions by email, and open
and track payments and product orders. It allegedly did exactly this
for the Maria Duval and Patrick Guerin letters, as well as for several
other psychic services that were also shut down by the US government.

Data Marketing Group's employees would open responses from
victims, take out the payments, and throw everything else in the en-

velope away—allegedly processing as much as $500,000 every two weeks. As soon as an individual payment was received, victims were then added to a comprehensive database, and new letters asking for additional payments were triggered, starting the cycle all over again. We imagined that the process within this concrete box looked something like that of an old-school factory assembly line.

Starting in May 2014, as money from victims continued to pour in, the company began being closely monitored by investigators. At one point, even its office trash cans were scoured for evidence. This glamorous Dumpster-diving mission was conducted by Thomas and several lucky colleagues. On three separate occasions, they staked out the Dumpsters outside the office building and dug through bags of rotting garbage, eventually recovering twenty-four boxes, or three weeks' worth of trash. Among all the debris, investigators found key pieces of evidence: twenty-two versions of the Maria Duval and Patrick Guerin solicitations, dozens of talismans, internal emails, business records, and around twenty thousand responses from victims, which included more than one hundred unsealed green envelopes full of photos and locks of hair (requested by Maria to allow her to feel victims' energy)— all of which ended up being integral to the government's case.

The discarded mementos the postal investigators retrieved gave the US government solid proof as to how these letters were a clear case of mail fraud. Instead of being used to establish psychic contact with Maria Duval as promised, all the heartfelt letters and special materials that victims sent in were being tossed out with half-eaten sandwiches and used coffee grounds. Not only that, but the supposedly personalized messages, lucky numbers, and predictions from these psychics were part of nearly identical form letters sent to millions. They differed only in the recipient's name and certain personal information placed throughout a carefully designed template.

"Destiny Research Center states clearly that the solicitation is derived from 'Duval's' or 'Guerin's' individual psychic vision about the consumer," Thomas said in his declaration. "When in fact Destiny Research Center is merely sending to consumers mass mailings of substantively identical solicitations containing identical visions."

The Business Web

I T WAS STARTING to become clear that what US investigators had called one of the most notorious mail frauds in history was hardly the work of one woman. Over the years, the scam had infiltrated countries all over the world: Japan, Italy, Denmark, Finland, Austria, Norway, New Zealand, Australia, the United States, Canada, and more. When one country shut it down, it quickly popped up in another.

Although the US government conducted a comprehensive investigation into the North American businesses involved in the worldwide scheme, it found that the roots of the letters went far deeper than the United States. And US investigators hadn't come close to pinpointing (at least publicly) the true brains behind this fraud, in large part due to the lack of enforcement power in other countries. In fact, we still couldn't find a government enforcement agency anywhere in the world that had been able to find the original source of the letters, as officials instead seemed to have zeroed in on nothing more than middlemen and fronts. Many of these governments hadn't even realized Maria Duval was a real person, something we now knew to be true. So we decided to try to find the masterminds of this unstoppable scheme ourselves, armed with nothing more than an oversize notepad and an already unhealthy obsession with Maria.

In our fluorescent-lit crowded New York City newsroom, we continued to pore through government documents, domain registries, and trademark applications, this time looking for the businesspeople behind the letters. We soon began to piece together a massive network, mapping out the players, companies, and connections on our giant notepad. Our crude map, covered in more than a dozen names, strikethroughs, different-colored highlights, and large question marks, looked like a CIA crime board out of a television show like *Homeland*. We were falling deeper and deeper down this rabbit hole, much to the confusion and curiosity of our coworkers.

At first it seemed to make little sense. There were so many different people. And so many different businesses. Slowly we began to notice patterns and overlaps among the many players in this decades-long operation. A wild cast of characters began to emerge as we scrawled name after name on a piece of paper.

Early in our investigation we were convinced that an Australian man by the name of Joseph Patrick Davitt and Listano Limited, the company he directed, were key to unlocking the mystery of Maria Duval. Listano's name appeared in the domain registrations of MariaDuval.com and MariaDuval.net, which became inactive shortly after we started our investigation. Listano was also listed as the current owner of the international trademarks for Maria's name—the same trademarks that had allegedly once been registered by the woman herself. This meant that it was now Joseph's firm, and not Maria, that had the ability to use the Maria Duval name for business purposes.

As we dug further, we considered whether Joseph—though never named in the US government action or convicted of any wrongdoing—might have had a role, whether intentional or not, in concealing the identity of the scam's real ringleaders. First we came

across his LinkedIn profile, which showed that he ran his own marketing firm in Australia. The firm's low-budget website featured a
smiling Joseph Davitt with short-cropped brown hair and dimples
wearing a white business shirt and tie. Next to his photo was the
outline of a kangaroo (in case we ever forgot he was based in Australia).

We were dying to talk to him, but our many efforts left us confused at best. We called his marketing firm. He quickly answered the
phone by saying, "Joe Davitt," but the line went silent as soon as we
mentioned we were reporters looking for Maria Duval. After hanging on the line for a minute or so in silence, he hung up entirely. We
called back multiple times only to get a recording in a woman's voice.
Within weeks, his firm's website had gone down for maintenance
and eventually disappeared altogether. Then his LinkedIn profile
vanished.

A week later, the same woman's voice was on the answering machine, but the greeting had been changed to say we had reached Super-
Green Lawn Seed. A quick search for SuperGreen Lawn Seed revealed
a site for another one of Joseph's businesses, this one advertising a special lawn fertilizer supposedly designed for Australia's "harsh and con-
trasting climate." We were bewildered.

Later we found what appeared to be his most recent address. All
Google Street View showed us was a large, empty grass lot. Another
address, from an old business filing, seemed to be his actual home, a
large two-story, walled-in house with what looked like floor-to-ceiling
windows, balconies, and a three-car garage. Located only seven minutes away from his other address and a few miles from the beach, the
home was nestled in a small seaside town in Victoria, Australia. It
looked like a beautiful place to visit, and we would have loved to try to
confront him in person, adding to what would become a long list of all

the exotic reporting trips we could take for this investigation if only our budget allowed. Instead, we remained on the fifth floor of our New York high-rise emailing and calling him over the following months to no avail.

. . .

At a dead end, we gathered everything we could about the company that had led us to Joseph in the first place, Listano Limited. And that's when something peculiar emerged.

Listano's address was listed at 37 Greenhill Street in Stratford-upon-Avon. We both knew of Stratford-upon-Avon as a tourist destination famous for being Shakespeare's birthplace. Why, though, would an Australian business have a physical location in this quaint British town on an entirely different continent? Again we turned to Google Street View, which zeroed in on a nondescript building above a fabric store across the street from a kebab shop. The street looked like a mix of old and new, containing a noodle shop and cell phone store housed in traditional Tudor-style and classic redbrick buildings. We zoomed from every angle we could, searching for a sign.

No Listano in sight.

We started to figure out that something suspicious might be going on when the UK company registry database showed that more than one hundred businesses were registered to that very same address. As we scrolled through the names of the different companies, we saw some very familiar people listed as directors. Andrea Egger, the attorney from Maria's trademark applications, was named on filings for an investment company listed at 37 Greenhill Street. Meanwhile, Martin Dettling, the man who'd opened the Sparks mailboxes, was listed as a former director of a "helisports and megayacht" company at the same address.

Why were so many businesses listed at this same odd address even when there didn't appear to be a single company in sight? And why were so many of them somehow connected to Maria Duval? Someone had to be behind it. But who?

That's when we found a curious accountant named Barney Mc-Gettigan. His accounting firm was one of the companies listed at the address, so we decided to try giving him a call. A cheerful British man answered the phone and confirmed that his office was the only business physically located at 37 Greenhill Street. When we explained that we were looking for a company called Listano Limited because of its ownership of Maria Duval's websites and trademarks his tone quickly shifted.

We couldn't record the call, but here's how we remembered it from our notes.

US: *Do you work with Listano Limited?*

BARNEY: *Um, I'm not sure. Actually, I would have to look at our records to see what our association with them is.*

US: *Does this mean they aren't physically located there?*

BARNEY: *That's correct. We offer a service to some of our clients to allow them to use our office as a registered office.*

US: *We've seen a number of companies linked to the psychic Maria Duval that are registered at your address. Can we email you a list so that you can look them up in your records?*

BARNEY: *I'd rather not give you my email . . .*

After this, Barney ended the call with an enthusiastic "Righty-ho!" and quickly hung up the phone.

Confused, we did some research and learned that Barney must

be a registered agent, something that is surprisingly common in the business world. These agents help set up businesses and provide them with a physical address to use on public government filings. While these kinds of services are used by legitimate companies, they are also a perfect tool for criminals trying to remain in the shadows. Many fraudsters, we discovered, use registered agents to create so-called shell companies, fake businesses that have no real operations and are simply used to obscure the true nature of their activities.

But back to our call. Barney told us he would look into Listano and let us know what he found. We never did hear from him again.

It was still unclear whether or not Barney was directly linked to Maria or knew anything about her. He did help us solve one mystery, though. We finally knew who'd been helping to churn out all the apparent shell companies at 37 Greenhill Street.

• • •

It seemed that every person who was associated with the Maria Duval letters took us to a dozen more leads. So one day, we decided to hole up in a little conference room with our laptops and a single phone to begin the task of calling people in countries all over the world, in the hopes that someone would point us in the right direction.

Each time we got ready to dial a new number, we practiced our spiel, prepared our questions, and held our breath. Sadly, almost every other phone call was met with nothing more than the dreaded beep of a disconnected phone line. When the phone did actually ring and someone answered, we were often hung up on.

One of the first people we tried was a Danish representative for Maria, who was named in an online news article. According to the article, this man claimed that responses to the mailings from around the world were forwarded to Maria in France and that he had helped arrange the interview between Maria and the journalist who wrote this article.

An elderly-sounding man with a thick accent answered the phone. We told him we were looking for information about Maria Duval, and he quickly said he didn't know "the lady." But as we kept asking questions about her, he conceded that he had met her.

"No no no no," he said, when we asked if he represented Maria. "Nothing to do with that woman. Not at all. I don't want to talk about that. It is so many years ago. I am out of that business. Thank you very much, bye." We tried calling him back, but he didn't answer his phone again.

The angriest person we reached—perhaps in part because we woke him up in the middle of the night—was a man named Gerard du Passage. Jan Vanlangendonck, the Belgian journalist who had interviewed Maria in Paris, told us Gerard was his "first and important contact person" when he investigated the Maria Duval letters a number of years earlier. We first called a US number listed as Gerard's, but we instead reached a woman who said she was his ex-wife. She told us that Gerard had once lived in New York but that he now lived in Thailand with a new wife. She said that she and Gerard had been married for more than forty years, and that she didn't really know what he did for work. "He works with individuals, mainly in Europe," she said. She was about to give us his cell phone number when she stopped herself, saying she had better check with Gerard first. She told us to call her back in a couple of days to get the number, but she never answered her phone again.

Next we tried the number where Jan, the Belgian journalist, had reached Gerard, this one listed in the United Kingdom. But it turned out he was thousands of miles from England. We woke Gerard up at four a.m. in Thailand. Needless to say, he was not excited about talking with us. "I'm not going to answer any questions. I have no idea who you are, and I'm not going to talk about this on the telephone," he said, before hanging up. We followed up with an email and more calls, but he still didn't seem to want to talk to us.

By this point, as some of our calls reached people who spoke languages we did not, we became increasingly frustrated by our inability to even figure out if we were speaking to the right person. Between the language barriers, the layers of secrecy, and the sheer number of people involved, there seemed to be a new obstacle around every corner. We were starting to worry that we would never figure out who had created this monster scam.

The Sparks Connection

T HE SWISS MAN who had opened the Sparks mailboxes was also evading us.

Martin Dettling was named in the US government's lawsuit because of his role as the director of Destiny Research Center, the Hong Kong company that had been used to send out the letters most recently. We learned from the few sites online where his name surfaced that he was a seventysomething man from Zurich who was a director of a number of other apparent shell companies, including one for which Andrea Egger, the attorney from Maria's trademark applications, was also listed on its business filings. It also appeared that Martin was behind a website that allowed angry spouses to post photos and reports of infidelity.

Puzzled, we reached out to a number of possible relatives of his, listed in a decades-old obituary for what appeared to be Martin's brother. The only person from the obituary we managed to get in touch with was a woman who seemed to be Martin's niece. While she was eager to try to help us find him, she said that neither she nor her sister had any idea where he might be these days and knew little about him. She told us that her father had been born and raised in Switzerland but that he had come to the United States in 1929, leaving behind his younger brother, who she thought was Martin. "I only met him once in 1967 when our entire family vacationed in Switzerland," she said.

If her dates were accurate, then the Martin Dettling we were looking for wouldn't have even been born when her father had left Switzerland in 1929. Perhaps this Martin was that Martin's son? More confused than ever, we moved on from Martin for the time being. But down the road, when Martin's name kept resurfacing, we turned back to the obituary. We suddenly realized that we had glossed over a huge clue. That Martin's brother—or whoever he actually was—had died in Reno, Nevada.

When we had first read the obituary, we'd somehow overlooked this, but now we thought the Reno connection might shed some light on why those mailboxes had ended up in the tiny town of Sparks, less than a fifteen-minute drive away. The US government had found that Martin was the one who opened the mailboxes. Could it be that the reason he picked Sparks, of all places, was actually a lot less random than we'd first thought?

We quickly called her back. While she again said she knew next to nothing about Martin or why he would have opened these mailboxes in Nevada, she did tell us something very peculiar: Her father, from the obituary, hadn't actually died in Reno. Instead, he died in the middle of playing blackjack—at a casino in Sparks, Nevada.

The Whistleblower

WHISTLEBLOWERS HAVE ALWAYS been a journalist's best friend. Former employees are often the ones who know where all the bodies are buried. From our past investigations, we knew that they can also be far more willing to talk than someone who is actively involved with a company. Early on in our investigation into the Maria Duval letters, we blasted out dozens of messages to every person we could find who had ever worked at any of the key companies associated with the scam.

We started by looking for people who worked at Astroforce, a company listed in Maria's website domain history and as the publisher of many of her books. Astroforce seemed to be some sort of front company with filings in many different countries, so we weren't expecting an Astroforce employee to be the person to respond to our inquiry. But out of the blue and in the middle of the night, an email broke the investigation wide open.

When I discovered the system, I left. How can I help you?

We responded to the initial email with some specific questions, but this man wasn't yet ready to share what he knew.

I don't know who you are.

What do you want to do with these [*sic*] info?

What do you already know?

What is your goal?

Please tell me more.

Once we finally convinced him to get on the phone, he spoke with us at length. He became tangled up in the Maria Duval scam after accepting what seemed like a great marketing job. All these years later, he was still so nervous about being connected to the scheme or angering its creators that he insisted on remaining anonymous.

He went on to tell us the story of how this massive scam began, starting with two European businessmen in a small luxe town in Switzerland. Showing clear knowledge of the inner workings of the con, he described in detail the way the Maria Duval letters were set up to bombard victims with new solicitations based on how they responded.

He told us he had never met Maria but had seen her on TV once in Switzerland. He described her as "not a smart woman," and he suggested that in many ways Maria was a pawn in the scheme, having never even seen one of the many letters sent with her face and signature. "She received money for it, but she didn't know what kind of letters," he said.

When we asked how much money she was making, he said, "Absolutely no idea; I presume it was royalties or maybe a check at the end." He also told us he wasn't sure if she was still alive. And right away he turned the conversation away from Maria and told us to focus instead on the two European businessmen: a French "mailing genius" named Jacques Mailland and a Swiss business titan named Jean-Claude Reuille.

He said that Jean-Claude ran both Astroforce and a company called Infogest. (We already knew about a Canadian company named Infogest Direct Marketing from the US government lawsuit, which named it as the source of the US and Canadian letters. But it turned out that the company our whistleblower was telling us about was the Swiss parent company, officially known as Infogest SA.) Jean-Claude, our source told us, was careful to keep his name off official business filings but was definitely the leader of Infogest, which he said was in charge of the scam's global operations. And Jacques, he said, was the one who had created the story behind Maria for Infogest, which then allegedly exported the letters to companies around the globe to carry out in their own countries. This franchise-like model helped explain why we saw so many different companies connected to the very same letters. A government source would later describe the system to us as a "fraud in a box."

The whistleblower told us that because of Maria's growing reputation as a psychic who could find missing people, Jacques had decided to hire her to be the face and name of his new mailing campaign in the early nineties, along with two other purported psychics. He said that there was a time when the letters were sent from all three psychics. But it was Maria who became the superstar.

Our source had worked at Astroforce in the nineties. He had heard that the company shut down years ago, which was why he was surprised to hear that the scheme was still in action. "[There] should be some very rich people behind it," he said.

It was hard to contain our excitement while speaking with him. Not only did he give us some juicy new details, but he was adamant that Jacques and Jean-Claude were somehow at the center of this.

Their names were not new to us. Even before our interview with this employee, our investigation of public documents had revealed a trail backing up the idea that these two men were extremely important to the Maria Duval operations.

Yet if Jacques and Jean-Claude were the original masterminds, were they still in charge? Or had they handed off the operations? What were they up to now?

The "Mailing Genius"

W E WERE MOST intrigued by what our whistleblower said about Jacques, the Frenchman who he claimed had turned Maria into the international sensation she was today. We already knew Jacques had long been associated with the Maria Duval letters, and, more important, he appeared to have a direct line to Maria herself, with Jan Vanlangendonck, the journalist from Belgium, telling us that Jacques called himself Maria's "secretary" and had arranged the 2007 interview in the Paris hotel.

From what the former employee, and later a number of other people who had worked with him over the years, told us, Jacques was a copywriter. It was his job to create the content that would entice people to buy "products." But instead of writing letters selling vacuum cleaners or furniture, Jacques made his money from psychic mailings. "Jacques Mailland is a famous direct marketing copywriter in the world of psychics," another anonymous source told us much later in our hunt. This man, who claimed to have been involved with the Maria Duval business in France, remembered Jacques living in New York in the mid-1990s, where he translated piles of the Maria letters. He told us how Jacques and a colleague would recruit well-known psychics for these kinds of scams, convincing them to sign something called a "notoriety exploitation contract" so that their name and photos could be used on letters.

We also discovered an online bio saying Jacques was once a psychotherapist, and we found that he'd written a book in 1998 titled *Connais-toi toi-même*, which roughly translates to "Know thyself."

Most of the information that showed up online about Jacques was from a long time ago. We looked for more recent information about him on social media and found a profile picture of a lanky man with deep-set eyes, graying hair, and yellow teeth wearing a white tank top and grinning widely. His Facebook profile showed us all the different groups or pages he had liked, and these included a Brazilian restaurant, the beach town of São Miguel do Gostoso, a series of short films about a Normandy farmhouse in the year 2050, a flying car company in the Netherlands, and a French website dedicated to high-end watches. Other photos from his profile showed him with his grandchildren and kitesurfing and relaxing in Brazil, leaving us to wonder if this was even the right man.

With what felt like glorified stalking, a crucial part of our day-to-day job as reporters, we were able to find a few clues that this lanky man was indeed the Jacques we were looking for and that he might still be involved in Maria's operations. His Google+ profile, for example, showed a connection to a name we recognized: Maria's psychic sidekick Patrick Guerin. Was Patrick, the Parisian psychic, Jacques's latest success story?

An online list of attendees of a 2013 marketing conference held in the resort town of Marbella, Spain, included Jacques Mailland as a representative of a Swiss firm that we'd seen on a number of recent copyright registrations for Maria Duval ads in Russia and Ukraine. This wasn't your average trade conference. Held in ritzy

destinations around the world, it was an annual event at which people and businesses associated with a number of mailing schemes all
convened.

Jacques's name had also been on the radar of other journalists.
When a Dutch reporter named Willem Bosma got in touch with us,
he shared a wealth of information from his own investigation back
in 2007. He spoke with us over the phone at length after work one
evening from his desk at the newspaper where he worked in the
Netherlands. We frantically tried to take notes and interpret what
he was saying through his thick accent as he spoke excitedly about
all of his own frustrations and discoveries that were rushing back
to him. He was told at the time that Jacques worked closely with
Maria.

One of the people who told Willem about Jacques was the angry
man whom we'd woken up by calling him in Thailand, Gerard du
Passage. "I called him up in London and he said don't call me, call
Jacques Mailland," Willem said, recounting that Gerard had told him
that Jacques handled any press interest. "I asked, 'What do you want
with this business?' And du Passage said churches do that too. [He
said that] although churches want to make money, they bring a lot of
good things to people like we do." Gerard also warned Willem that
landing an interview with Maria would be "nearly impossible." "She
has been too often disappointed," he told Willem.

Willem heard about Jacques again, from a different businessman
involved with the scheme. "If you want to contact Maria Duval,
please ask Jacques Mailland," the man told Willem at the time. "He is
her personal secretary. She loves giving interviews, as she likes publicity."

For Willem, actually getting to Jacques wasn't as easy as Gerard
and the businessman made it sound. Willem was given his name

and contact information only after calling all the companies connected to the scheme in the Netherlands and insisting that he needed to talk to someone in charge. When he did finally reach Jacques by phone, he said that Jacques acknowledged his involvement with the Maria Duval operations, referring to himself as Maria's personal secretary and website manager. And, from Willem's recollection, the Frenchman didn't seem to think he was doing anything wrong:

"He said, 'Who could be against it? That we put people in the position to feel better than they did. Even medics recognized the placebo effect exists and can have a healing role.'"

There were even more telling quotes in the years-old notes from Willem's call with Jacques, which he was nice enough to share with us. "In a way it is our purpose to make money, but life improvement is a higher purpose. . . . You have true people and you have crooks," Jacques had said to him. "When you don't use an ethical standard, your business doesn't last. When you cheat people, that is wrong. We have everyone refunded, if they aren't satisfied with our products."

All these years later, Willem was still disturbed by how these men were able to justify such a heartless scheme so easily—and get away with it. "It's a world that I've never come across in my work," he told us.

We too tried to speak with Jacques. Over and over again. Desperate to track him down, we called every phone number we could find, at one point speaking with an angry woman who yelled at us in French, and almost every other time hearing the familiar sound of a disconnected line. We emailed a number of possible addresses with no luck. We obsessively monitored his Facebook page, looking for any new posts. And we even contacted women who appeared to be his daughters.

We were left with nothing but silence. Until this.

From: ███████████████████████
Sent: Monday, December 07, 2015 12:22 PM
To: Ellis, Blake
Subject: Re: Looking for Jacques Mailland

Hello
Sorry but he is dead!!!
He had an accident in France tin [*sic*] may.

It was a Monday in early December, almost two months into our hunt, and we were just planning to grab lunch when this message appeared in our inbox.

It came from a Brazilian kitesurfing school we'd contacted as a last resort after seeing photos of Jacques on its Facebook page. We'd never expected to hear back.

Sitting next to each other at our newsroom desks, we stared at our computer screens in disbelief. Jacques Mailland, the man we were so desperate to speak with, was dead? And he'd died just months before we started trying to reach him?

News of his death was quickly corroborated by one of his business colleagues who was unaffiliated with the Brazilian kitesurfing school. He was someone whom we'd emailed during our earlier stalking phase, before learning of his death. "Sadly Mr. Mailland died in a motorbike accident in May this year," he wrote. This business associate later told us the accident occurred outside Paris, and that the funeral took place on May 7, 2015. For weeks we tried to find an accident report or other official record of his death but were unsuccessful.

There were so many questions we wanted to ask Jacques, like how such a seemingly fun-loving family man could be involved in such a heartless scheme.

Whether he was dead or alive, we would never know for sure.

The Bizarre Businessman

THE OTHER PERSON we believed was central to the scheme was Jean-Claude Reuille. Aside from learning that he was still alive and living in Thailand with a new wife, our online sleuthing and interviews with those who had worked with him revealed a very peculiar individual.

Jean-Claude was a serial entrepreneur who hawked all kinds of weird products reminiscent of those on late-night television infomercials: shoe insoles that help you lose weight, a device that instantly ages wine, a little box that can heat an entire home, a knife that can cut anything, an asparagus pill that helps dieters shed pounds immediately, and a breast-firming cream.

When it came to the Maria Duval letters, he hadn't been in the public eye like Jacques, and we'd been told he'd conveniently kept his name off key business filings. He had also managed to steer clear of any of the government actions we had come across and was never named or convicted of any wrongdoing. But there were just too many connections between Jean-Claude and the businesses and people involved with the scam, down to office buildings, attorneys, auditors, and a curly-haired Colorado copywriter, for them all to be mere coincidences. The various clues we were able to dig up indicated that this man had long been in the shadows of the operation. Most telling of all was the fact that Infogest, which had publicly acknowledged its direct involvement with the letters, had once clearly been owned by Jean-Claude.

The weirdest stuff came from an article in a Swiss magazine, *L'Hebdo*, from 1994—around the same time we were told that Jacques had hatched the Maria Duval mail scheme, allegedly for Jean-Claude's company.

Jean-Claude Reuille is a happy and feel-good kind of guy— because he is a user of all his products. At 44, he demonstrates surprising sexual vitality due to the guarana remedies that he sells. He is never in pain, thanks to his pain-relief bracelet. He is constantly losing weight due to his Dr. Metz shoes, which he also sells. In his cellar, bottles age five to ten years in only 20 seconds, thanks to a light tube made by one of his companies.

Jean-Claude Reuille is a generous guy: he wants to share with all Swiss the things that have contributed to his happiness. "I only sell a product once I deem it good for my clients."

This is how the article, which was published in French, starts out. From there, it goes on to tell a story of a spiritual man who found huge success through selling these New Age products, with its author citing supposed annual revenue figures of 41 million francs (or a little less than $30 million US dollars at the time) from three of his companies, which seemed to us to be an astronomical figure for someone selling such random products.

The trinkets of happiness are in high demand. Jean-Claude Reuille hasn't always been this happy. When he was only 20

years old, sick of living in a narrow-minded and petty coun-
try, Reuille left for the United States. "I learned simple rules to
achieve my personal goals." Shortly after arriving, he became
a member of the Raelian movement and communicated with
aliens before coming back to earth and launching his business
career.

Huh? All these business ventures were already crazy enough.
Now aliens were involved?

With a quick Google search we learned that Raelism is a "UFO
religion" centered on the belief that humans descended from aliens.
The group claims to have more than 85,000 members in 107 countries, and its website boasts a swastika-inspired Star of David as a
logo, though the group says the image symbolizes peace. The movement is led by a man named Rael, who has an equally colorful biography.

At the age of 27, on the morning of December 13, 1973, while
he was still leading his successful racing-car magazine, RAEL
had a dramatic encounter with a human being from another
planet, at a volcano park in the center of France, known as "Puy
de Lassolas." This extra-terrestrial gave him a new detailed ex-
planation of our origins and information on how to organize our
future. . . . After six consecutive meetings in the same location,
Rael accepted the mission given to him, to inform humanity of
this revolutionary message and to prepare the population to wel-
come their Creators, the Elohim, without any mysticism or fear,
but as conscious and grateful human beings. After a few months
considering this huge task, Rael almost developed a stomach
ulcer before finally deciding to give up his much loved career as

a sports-car journalist and devote himself fully to the task as-signed to him by Yahweh—the extra-terrestrial whom he met.

Curious to know how long Jean-Claude had been a member of this supernatural religion, we searched around and discovered that his name was listed in 2001 as the publisher of a Rael book, *Yes to Human Cloning: Eternal Life Thanks to Science.*

We also stumbled on Swiss government filings that showed Reuille owned his own publishing business, offering such titles as *Le massage erotique.* The Swiss magazine article discusses this company as well, detailing the kinds of books that were being published and how this activity was just the beginning of Jean-Claude's growing reputation.

His books shed light on how to become a millionaire, how to memorize easily, how to communicate, how to master the power of your subconscious, and how to perform erotic massage for couples. Jean-Claude Reuille doesn't stop there. In 1989, his name spread around the world. He's the businessman who bought a page in the daily "La Suisse" to invite the woman of his dreams to a weekend of her dreams. The editor received over 500 letters in response.

The article takes a more skeptical tone from there, detailing how chemists in the Swiss town of Nyon complained that Jean-Claude's water purifier ads were wrongly convincing residents in the area that the municipal tap water wasn't safe to drink. It also describes how a consumer filed a complaint in Switzerland about false advertising surrounding Jean-Claude's "healing stones," which his ads claimed would "make disappear most health problems without any medication, diet, or treatment to follow."

Jean-Claude didn't seem fazed. "It's not in my interest to sell junk, because my expenses are much higher if my customers are unhappy," the magazine quotes him as saying. "The county doctors, the county pharmacists, the Office of Drug Control (OICM), they are constantly bothering me. These good people are mistakenly attacking me, because I don't set out to heal; what I do is prevention."

More details about Jean-Claude would come from a man who had worked for him in Switzerland but claimed no involvement with the Maria Duval letters. He told us that Jean-Claude lived in a villa on La Côte, "the best coast in Switzerland." Located on the north shore of Lake Geneva, La Côte is famous for its lush vineyards and mountain views. Jean-Claude's house, he told us, was "all white, clean, and strange."

"He was a strange guy," the former employee said, telling us that he wasn't surprised to hear that Jean-Claude could be wrapped up in such a massive scam. "I remember every Sunday, he was working all day. He drove his Mercedes. The car was always there," the source told us. "It was always kind of shadowy. There was always a shadow around the whole thing. It was all really hardly legal. They operated on the edge of what's legal."

• • •

We needed to talk to Jean-Claude.

We tried to call him at every number we could find. Most were disconnected, and one led us to a generic French voice mail. After we'd just about given up on ever reaching him, we received an email from the man himself. He was responding to a written letter we'd sent halfway around the world to his beachfront villa in Thailand, where we'd discovered he had moved almost a decade earlier.

To our surprise, he was very friendly and courteous. He claimed to be severely misunderstood. His email contained a confusing list of what he called "biographical facts," including an assertion that he hadn't had any contact with Raelism since 1989. But one thing was clear: he was adamant that he was "NOT" involved in a business with Maria Duval or any other psychic. He wouldn't provide a phone number where we could reach him, saying English wasn't his first language and he didn't want to be taken out of context. He did agree, however, to answer some of our questions by email.

We compiled a long list of all the connections we'd found and asked him to explain how he could possibly claim to be uninvolved, pointing out that Infogest (his company) even admitted to representing Maria Duval's business operations in 2005. In his reply email, he acknowledged that Infogest had once been one of his companies, but he said he had given up his management role many years ago and officially retired in 2006. He remained insistent that he had nothing to do with the Maria Duval letters.

> Waow, you've been told a lots of stories . . .
>
> . . .
>
> I will repeat what I told you previously: I was never involved with Maria Duval business.
>
> I used to travel quite a lot and I used to meet all kind of people including players from the Mail Order Industrie [sic].
>
> Jacques Mailland and Maria Duval were part of them.
>
> They used to travel the world together and I had the chance to share a few lunch or Dinner with them. If I remember correctly, the last one was long time ago in Paris.
>
> However, they never worked for me and they never been on any payroll of any of my companies.

If I remember correctly, they were part of a Group named Astroforce. . . .

I guess it would be easier for you if I would take full responsibility
for the Worldwide Mail Order Industry.

But, I'm only willing to take credit for what I did and nothing else.

All the best,

JC

We still couldn't believe we were emailing back and forth with
this man. He even acknowledged he had had dinner with Maria and
Jacques, conjuring up a million images in our heads of the trio toasting their success and chuckling over fancy bottles of French wine
and escargot. While we still believed he was involved with the scam,
it seemed plausible that he had left it behind years ago to enjoy a
cushy retirement in paradise.

It was Willem, the Dutch journalist, who eventually gave us
solid proof that we had been right about Jean-Claude all along. Willem sent us a copy of an official business filing showing that for a
short time in 2002, Jean-Claude himself was listed on public documents as an official shareholder of the Dutch firm previously known
as Astroforce. This was the company linked to the letters at which
our whistleblower worked, the same company Jean-Claude had
claimed had nothing to do with him. Willem had held on to a filing
that he'd received from the government years ago. Jean-Claude was
usually careful to keep his name out of things, presumably so he
could deny any involvement whatsoever. He or someone he worked
with must have slipped up.

Months later, when we eventually published this information in
a story online, Jean-Claude resurfaced.

Would you be kind enough to send me a copy of this Dutch business fillings [*sic*]?

As I do not see how this could be possible, I would really like to investigate.

Thank you for your cooperation.

The document he requested was public, so we were happy to oblige. Then Jean-Claude went quiet. And with that, our relationship with him was over. Perhaps he'd had no idea that this public connection existed.

We were convinced we would never hear from him again.

The Copywriter

A S WE DUG deeper into the business web behind the millions of letters sent around the world, we learned that much of their power was the work of "mailing geniuses" like Jacques Mailland, the copywriters behind the stories that hooked victims over and over again.

The US government's lawsuit contained copies of the letters that went on for pages and pages, using strategically placed details from the recipient's own lives, such as his or her name, age, and birthday. The letters wove intricate tales of Maria's history and adventures as a psychic with predictions of the wonderful fortunes that awaited the victim when he or she responded. They also played heavily on their readers' emotions, painting Maria as a trusted friend and adviser who could fill whatever void they had in their lives.

No matter what letter you picked up, Maria was telling you how she understood you and was there for you. She was always relatable, detailing concerns and events from her own life that elderly, sick, or lonely recipients could have been experiencing too. She was then always quick to provide the perfect solution. "You must no longer go on wearing a blindfold, as if you were in a fog, without knowing what the future holds for you. You are 86 years old, and you still have many years ahead of you," she said in one letter uncovered by USPIS investigators. "Don't say: 'I've missed the boat.' . . . From this point on, I want you to know I am your friend and I share what you are feeling. I sincerely think you have enormous strengths WITHIN YOURSELF of which you are unaware, or which you do not know how to use to the maximum. You also have a big heart, but you are often misunderstood by those around you."

Poring over countless examples of these letters from over the years, we became increasingly curious about the people, the copywriters, who had actually written them. How do you even find a job like this? Did these copywriters realize they were part of an international scam? How did they sleep at night, knowing that everything originated with these very letters? Did they view it just like any other copywriting job, such as writing advertising copy for a magazine or catalog? Or did working on the Maria Duval letters pay so well that the money made it possible to look past the rest?

Unable to speak with Jacques, we were thrilled when we were actually able to find one of the many people who had written some of the letters that had gone out in Maria's name. A middle-aged Canadian man with glasses and a friendly smile told us he had worked for countless mailing operations. He was surprisingly candid with us and willing to answer all of our questions as long as we didn't reveal his identity.

He started out by telling us that before he'd gotten wrapped up in the world of lucrative mail-order copywriting, he had been a journalist just like us. He was a radio and television news reporter for a decade, he said, picking up assignments from his bureau and then heading straight to the police station before setting off to cover three-alarm fires, murders, and other horrific news events, always with his police scanner in tow. "After going to my 187th fatal fire where four children were killed, I didn't want to be in a war zone anymore," he said.

One day he spotted an ad for an international marketer. Confident in his writing and storytelling abilities, he applied for the job, which turned out to be for a direct-mailing agency. He interviewed with the president of the company, but after forty-five minutes of talking, he was told that the position had already been filled. He was asked, however, if he had ever written advertising copy. At his old job, he'd jotted down the occasional ad script to be read over the radio airwaves, so he said, "Sure." With that, the president handed him a letter that at the time was being used to sell lottery tickets by mail. "Rewrite this," the president directed.

"So I rewrote the letter. He crumpled it up, and threw it in the garbage and said, 'When can you start?'"

He'd been a copywriter ever since. We asked him how difficult it had been to make the transition from reporting important, fact-based news to creating made-up, fantastical stories in an attempt to solicit money. To our surprise, he didn't seem to see as much of a distinction as we did. "When I worked as a reporter, I was in the storytelling business, just like I am now," he told us. "My stories used to be 'Main Street is on fire, here's an interview with the man who just lost everything.' Now my storytelling is more, 'Once upon a time, long, long ago on a planet far, far away. . .'"

He started out writing letters and manuals all related to the sale of overseas lottery tickets. But soon he was taking on all kinds of assignments, from lip plumpers to diet pills, all with the same goal: to convince people that whatever he was advertising was about to change their lives. "I was taught very early that I never sell products, I sell solutions. I'm always selling the dream, in other words," he said.

"I'm going to tell you both to close your eyes and just imagine how great it's going to feel when all your brand-new furniture is loaded up in the new truck and you're moving to a new neighborhood and waving goodbye to the neighbors you hate."

The jobs where he could really let his creativity and writing juices flow were for psychics like Maria. These writing jobs let him impersonate someone completely new and get into character each time he sat at his desk.

"I wrote one for a psychic: 'Did you feel it? Last night, actually early this morning, maybe two or two thirty, it was like a cold breeze went over my body. Did you feel that? If you did, it's possible we shared a psychic experience.'"

He once wrote about how Maria would stay up all night thinking about the recipient, and about how she was hearing voices from guardian angels. "The guardian angel told me something specific about you that you need to know—send me 25 dollars and I'll tell you the same secrets that the guardian angel whispered in my ear," he remembered writing.

For another letter, this one on behalf of Maria, he asked recipients to place their own hand on a drawn outline of a hand, saying Maria had become so flooded with work that she had gathered a team to help her analyze the energy from the handprint. We had seen a letter a lot like the one he was describing within the government lawsuit—with the outline of a hand and instructions for recipients to place their own hand on top. "So that I can get a sample of your vibrations and energy, please place your hand upon the image below and count slowly to 7," it stated.

He received many requests to write these kinds of letters as the mail-order psychic business boomed in the nineties. He wrote Maria Duval letters for two entirely different companies, in two different countries, most recently flying to Russia to help write letters for her around five years ago. Of all the psychics he wrote letters for, he said that Maria Duval was the only one that had grown into a true franchise, with different operations pumping the letters out from different locations.

Explaining how he determined whether his work had been successful, he told us that some of his best letters hooked at least 10 percent of those they had gone out to, while a dud would receive a response only 3 or 4 percent of the time. He said that while some copywriters liked to work on a royalty basis, receiving ten cents for every dollar that came in as a result of their letter, for example, he sometimes chose to receive a flat fee for his services.

He claimed that his work was all about delivering his recipients a masterfully told story, without making specific promises he knew could not be kept. He explained that he was one of many Maria Duval copywriters, and that each one had his or her own style. While some letters crossed the line, such as those boasting that the recipient would win thousands of dollars the next day, he claimed he never did that. "I know that's illegal because I'm promising something you can't deliver," he told us. He said he had also turned down jobs when he learned a specific letter would go only to people in their nineties.

"I started raising my rates to the point where they couldn't afford me." He would tell agencies his fee was $100,000, he said, about a job for which he would have previously charged $20,000. " 'I have to have money for the bail and the lawyer; I need to have that up front.' " This would always scare them off, he said.

He also claimed that some of the best mailers he had worked with refused to send letters to addresses of people over a certain age, and they would cut off recipients who sent too much money. "There are mailers who have the conscience to say, 'Hey I'll take a nickel from everyone, but I won't suck a person dry.' " Other companies he worked for kept a list he described as "don't ever mail them again," which contained the names of those who demanded that they be left alone, those who informed the sender that whoever the letter was trying to reach was dead, and those who preferred to receive money first before sending any of their own to a psychic.

Our hunch was that this sympathetic side of the business probably had more to do with avoiding authorities, such as officials who might be tipped off by a well-meaning bank employee or family member, than with any sort of moral compass. But this perspective was interesting nonetheless. It showed how easy it was for a person inside this business, whether a copywriter or someone at the helm of an operation, to justify the work he or she did. As Jacques had told Willem, the Dutch journalist, "you have true people and you have crooks." "When you cheat people, that is wrong," he had said, apparently convinced that all the people receiving Maria's letters were happy with the attention they were getting and how the letters made them feel, something Maria herself had echoed in interviews.

"The first thing they get is a nice warm and fuzzy feeling that someone still writes to them," the Canadian copywriter told us, agreeing with the idea that the good these letters do can outweigh the bad. The desperation among recipients is also what makes the letters so successful, he explained. "Because when Mrs. Jones, who's seventy-five, when the kids are gone and grandkids are gone . . . and the first thing [she reads] is [her] name. [She thinks], 'It's so nice that somebody writes to me.' That's the number one thing."

"You do get people who say, 'I'm so glad you contacted me—I'm at the end of the tether,'" he said. "You realize, all these people want is a friend. . . . Yeah, I shouldn't be talking to people, but where are their kids, where are their friends? Why aren't they talking to them? You go to a senior community and see how many people never leave their room. Those are the people I'm going to mail to because they need a friend."

"Do you ever feel bad about doing any of this?" we asked.

"Yes, to an extent," he said, "but at the same time, I'm sorry, but I think I'm doing good and giving people someone to talk to. If they didn't talk to me they would talk to someone else—and hopefully someone legitimate, but I can't control that."

Still, he acknowledged that the letters didn't always have such noble intentions. "The biggest fear of women over age seventy is falling and breaking a hip. So a psychic will always say, 'You need my advice so you don't run into any medical catastrophes.' I know what your fear is. Am I playing on it? Yes. You learn ways to spin your tale and spin your yarn so that they say, 'I'm going to get something out of this.'"

He was also well aware that many of the people receiving his letters were a little too gullible, telling us the story of a woman who sent back her order form with her American Express Platinum card attached. With it came a note explaining that she couldn't figure out how to fill out the order form, so could they please do it for her and send her card back when done? "I never look at it as 'These people are too stupid to live.' That said, you would be amazed at the stupid stuff people will do," he said.

He even gave us a glimpse into his writing process for each letter, saying that he drew on his broadcast reporting skills, writing letters in an active voice that begged to be read aloud. "I sit down and I close my eyes and I compose it in my head and then I start to type," he began. "I will write the whole thing, a four-page letter, an eight-page letter, and then I walk away and the next day I'll read it out loud to myself and notice places I'm not strong enough. . . . [I'll] make changes, and it's done.

"A lot of writers go over a hundred drafts; they bleed over every word. I don't do that."

We asked him whom exactly he was writing these letters to, envisioning him sitting at his laptop and getting into his Maria Duval character.

He answered us quickly, rattling off a detailed answer. "She's about sixty-five, she's widowed, she probably has four or five kids; [she] may even have grandkids. She lives alone in a small apartment, lives on a small pension. She's not educated, but understands her world, probably thinks she didn't get the right breaks at the right time. . . . What I'm going to convince her is that Maria's going to make the rest of her days easier. It's been a hard sixty-five years. I'm gonna make it easier."

We immediately thought of Doreen.

The Nucleus

THE MARIA DUVAL letters may have been written by all sorts of copywriters over the years, but we were at least sure that they'd started with Infogest, the Swiss company that Jean-Claude had founded all those years ago.

Near the end of our international calling spree, we spoke with a man named Lukas Mattle, who had once been listed on business filings as a director of Infogest. It appeared that Lukas had gone on to run a driving school, whose website featured a witch on a broomstick with wheels and the motto "Driving Is No Witchcraft."

We gave him a call to see what he knew.

Lukas was driving through the mountains of Switzerland and his cell phone was going in and out of service so it took several dropped calls to get through to him. He spoke very little English, but we were able parse out something that piqued our interest. He said that he had worked at Infogest for a while but that the company—and Maria—were "finished."

We quickly started peppering him with more questions. What did he mean by "finished"? Did this mean Infogest was out of business? And if so, how were the Maria Duval letters still being sent out? Unfortunately, he was either playing dumb or had no idea what we were saying, because all he would say was "I don't know"—even when we asked him if he could understand us.

We tried to confirm this new information on our own. We called Infogest's Swiss telephone number, and the line was disconnected. A more comprehensive search of business records showed that the company was indeed liquidated in 2014, the same year of the US government's lawsuit. So who was calling the shots now if Infogest was "finished," and Jacques and Jean-Claude really were out of the picture?

As we returned home from work each night, we found it nearly impossible to quiet our racing minds. Out to dinner with family, watching TV, walking to the subway, at the gym, we would recheck our email on our phones, desperately hoping for the clue we had been waiting for. The holidays were approaching, but it was hard for us to think of anything else but our investigation. No longer outside observers, we were living fully inside this alternate universe full of conmen and shell companies. Before and after work, and all throughout the weekends, we emailed and texted back and forth constantly with each new theory that popped into our heads. Our loved ones were also wrapped up in the mystery, since it was all we could talk about. They were eager for us to find answers as each new crazy story or clue emerged.

We decided to turn to the most recent traces of Maria and the letters, searching for any proof of letters that had gone out since the US lawsuit was filed in 2014. This led us to Russia, where we found a flurry of Maria Duval activity: complaints, news articles, and, most notably, a Russian website offering psychic guidance. Using a much different template from her US websites, this site, with a muted purple background, featured a doctored version of one of the photos on Flickr from her Russian press conference (in which she was wearing the same chunky necklace and black, cleavage-baring top), next to an astrological chart. Across the top of the page was a toll-free number people could call to supposedly reach the clairvoyant, and there was an online form asking for personal information and how Maria could help, whether it be with money, wealth, or health.

There was also a page full of testimonials, which featured photos of real people next to each glowing review. Curious who these people were, we used a tool that allowed us to search images on Google that indicated where each specific image had appeared online. These cheesy photos were nothing more than stock images.

All of these traces of Maria Duval in Russia led us back to Jacques.

As we discovered earlier, a number of copyrights had recently been filed for Maria Duval ads in Russia and Ukraine. Listed as the registrant for these copyrights was the same company that Jacques had represented two years earlier at the shady marketing conference in Marbella, Spain, before his untimely death. It was also the same company listed as the most recent contact for Maria's US website.

To gather more information, we decided to call a man named Lucio Parrella, who appeared to work at the company. We were surprised when he acknowledged that he currently sold rights to Maria Duval's books, yet he also claimed to have nothing to do with Jacques and to know nothing about her letters. When we asked why his company's email address was listed as the contact for Maria's website, he said he had no idea and was working on getting it removed. Then he let it slip that Jacques might have been the one to put it there.

We were finally starting to form what seemed to be a very plausible theory: If Jean-Claude really had retired in 2006 as he'd said, maybe Jacques was the one who'd kept the scheme going for practically another decade. And with Jacques so recently deceased, it was quite possible that there wasn't anyone in charge anymore.

Much of the evidence we'd seen of letters going out, from online complaints and trademark filings to news reports, was from before Jacques's death. This left us wondering what Jacques's death meant for the future of the letters. And for Maria.

One thing was clear: many of the people we tracked down seemed to be nothing more than cogs in this massive machine. It was likely that their involvement in the scheme earned them money, even if it was simply being paid to put their names on official filings. These were the people used to keep investigators at bay, the fall guys if the ship went down.

It was no wonder that this was such an impossible case for law enforcement agencies to solve. There were so many companies. And so many people. And the money and the letters seemed to have gone through an endless number of hands. The Maria Duval "fraud in a box" had been passed around the world for decades, leaving valuable letter templates in the hands of an unknown number of people and operations. Now, with no clear leader, copycats appeared to be out there who used crude copies of images and letters found online to perpetrate their own versions of the scam.

We were confident that the Maria Duval scheme had started decades ago with two enterprising businessmen who were no longer the nucleus of the operation. Yet as we packed away our large notepad with the sprawling business web scrawled across it, we knew the story wasn't over. Maria was very much a real woman out there somewhere. But we still knew little about why she'd let herself get caught up in such a heartless fraud. Was it money? Love? Ego?

It was with her that our journey began, and it was with her that it must end. We needed to uncover the real story of the psychic herself.

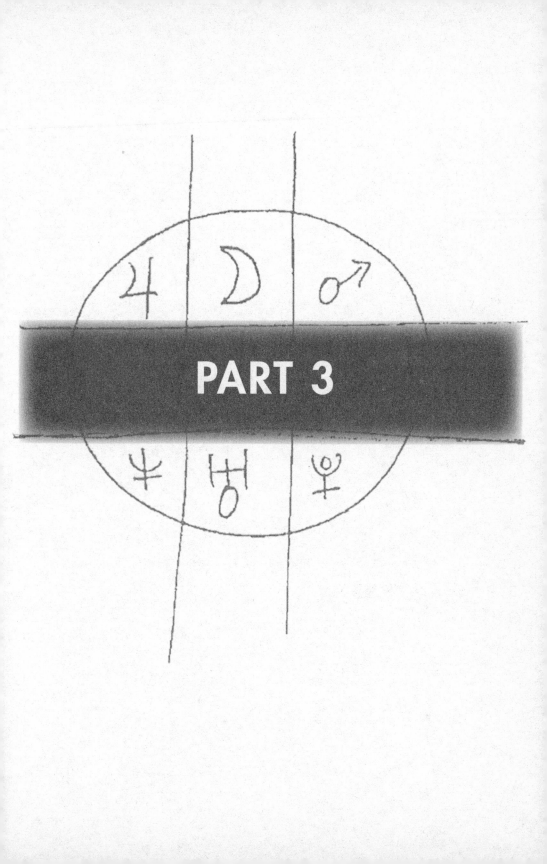

PART 3

The Windfall

W E STARTED WITH the same French address we had seen over and over again.

So many people had been adamant that Maria Duval was real that we'd begun to wonder whether the address from all the trademark filings could really be her home address. We looked up the town of Callas to find it was populated by a mere 1,900 people—small enough that town officials ought to know whether she lived there.

We called the phone number listed for the town hall of Callas and asked the woman who answered whether she knew of a psychic in her town named Maria Duval. To our surprise, she immediately said yes. In fact, she gave us a new address for Maria and told us that she was usually home, so we should try reaching her there. The employee then informed us by email the next day that Maria had actually come into the town hall that week.

It all seemed too easy. With this pivotal new information, the only way to continue our hunt would be to go to France. To date, our luxurious reporting trips from past investigations together had taken us to Houston, Texas, to gather information about a predatory government debt collector and to Ferguson, Missouri, to investigate the town's failing justice system. We were sure that traveling to the South of France to look for a psychic would be a tough sell to our bosses.

Expecting our editors to laugh at the idea of sending two reporters to French wine country, we pitched the trip to them in December, two months after finding that strange letter from Patrick Guerin. Yet they turned out to be just as wrapped up in the mystery, agreeing that our traveling there was the only way to truly see the story through. Still in disbelief that we were actually going to France, we quickly booked our flight and hotel before our editors changed their minds.

Before we left, with the assistance of our French-speaking colleague Julia Jones, we made one last round of calls to anyone we thought might have information about this elusive woman. Of all the people we called, it was the former mayor of Callas who had the most information to share. Françoise Barre, who had been mayor for nineteen years, just also happened to have been Maria's personal secretary for a decade. "I'm a very realistic person. I'm an accountant; I took her appointments; I was her secretary," she told us. "I'm very prosaic. I was mayor of my small town for three mandates, and I think people see me as having a good head on my shoulders, I'm not one to tell tales."

Luckily for us, she had held on to quite a few entertaining memories from her time working with Maria. There was the motorcyclist whom Maria cured on the spot with her "power of radiesthesia," in which she would put her hand on a person's body and emanate heat. "One day a young man walked in, his whole body shaking profusely because he had been in a motorcycle accident and couldn't walk well," Françoise recounted to us. "She spent a great deal of time with him, almost an hour. He walked out of there walking normally, no tremors."

Then there was the story of a woman who was constantly in large amounts of debt, who would frequently call Maria's office in search of winning lottery numbers. Maria eventually told Françoise to stop answering her calls, saying that people who wanted a magical, instant fix for their troubles were a waste of her time. Plus, she told Françoise that she had already warned the woman that she needed to be careful with her money and advised her to take out a low-interest loan from her husband's company to pay off her debt. Then one December, the woman called again.

"She said, 'You know, I am out of money, my husband already took out a loan, and Christmas is around the corner, we need to buy gifts for the kids and make a nice, special meal,'" Françoise recalled. "I said, 'Listen up, lady. On Christmas, when you're poor, you eat potatoes.'"

"She hung up on me," Françoise said, laughing. "I know, because I've spent Christmases eating potatoes, and that's why I can say it."

Often the calls were much more serious—such as, Françoise claimed, when Maria solved a murder by phone. "Madame Duval never answered the phone directly, since she had a lot of people calling for her, so I did the filtering, if you will," Françoise started. "One day, I received a phone call that was different."

When she answered the phone, a woman who had never consulted with Maria was on the other line. As was customary, Françoise didn't let her speak to Maria. "But Maria was about six feet away from me, and said to me in an extraordinary fashion, 'Give me the phone, let me talk to this person.'"

"But Maria, they've never consulted with you," Françoise remembered telling her.

"That doesn't matter," Maria said adamantly.

So she transferred the call to Maria. According to Françoise, "I just heard Maria say 'Tell me, what's her name? What's her birthday? When did she disappear? And where?'"

On the phone was the mother of a girl named Catherine, who had gone missing in Versailles. "And then, I'll tell you, I remember like it was yesterday," said Françoise. "[Maria] hung up the phone, looked at me, and said: 'Françoise, this girl drowned. She was pushed into the water, and we will never see her again.'"

Françoise was devastated for the girl's family and, at the same time, fascinated by Maria's ability to connect with the unknown. "Oh, it was terrible! But just like that, she was so present in everything she said." Maria asked her to call the inspector in charge of the investigation "right away," but Françoise couldn't get ahold of him, so they sent a fax.

"She dictated the fax to me," Françoise recalled. "'Mr. Inspector, . . . young Catherine'—I don't remember her last name—'disappeared around Disneyland, near Paris, where she worked. After she left work, no one saw her again, her mother told me. I can tell you what I saw. I saw that she was thrown into the water, I saw that she is dead, and I saw a man of color, in his thirties, very sporty, throw her into the water.'"

This level of detail certainly must have gotten the inspector's attention, because Maria received a phone call not much later from the police. "I just heard Maria say, 'No, sir, I knew nothing about this story, I swear!'" It turned out, Françoise said, that the police were investigating "a thirty-two-year-old man of color who was a triathlete. And he was the last person who had been seen with her; he was some sort of fling or boyfriend."

Stories of adoring fans and miraculous discoveries reminded us of the claims in the letters and news articles we had seen. But still they seemed pretty fantastical to our skeptical ears. Françoise sure seemed to have bought into Maria's powers and even claimed to have witnessed them firsthand. She was also a close friend. Perhaps she was simply trying to keep the lucrative myth of Maria Duval alive.

She even sent us a book that Maria had supposedly written. We had seen a number of listings for Maria Duval's books everywhere from Amazon to eBay, with titles like *The Seven Secrets of the Initiated*, *Words of Power*, *Secret Instructions*, and *How to Energize and Harmonize Your Aura*. The one Françoise sent us was very simply titled *How to Become Psychic*, and it included a story relating exactly how Maria had become aware of her psychic gift. It all happened while her uncle, the same Italian priest mentioned in many of her letters, was on his deathbed.

It was three o'clock in the afternoon in the tiny northern Italian town of Ravenna, Maria wrote, when her uncle closed his eyes and a "supernatural peace" came over his face. His body was still except for his chest, which slowly rose and fell. Townspeople dressed in black came from all over, camping out in the streets and visiting him at his bedside, where they whispered prayers and kissed his forehead before tiptoeing away. "They came from the mountains as soon as they heard that the father, the saint, was suffering."

When night fell, he awoke and asked for his teenage niece, Maria, who was fetched by one of the nuns. "I was at the office, having dinner," she wrote. "The nun took me by the hand. I followed her to the stairs and I remember hearing my heartbeat in my chest, as we climbed each step. I was at the cusp of a crucial discovery, a revelation, and I felt it."

When Maria showed up in his room, he asked her to come closer and sit on his bed. "It's you who holds the 'power' for the generation after mine," her uncle told her, according to the book. "Look closely into my eyes, they are just like yours, green and speckled with yellow dots. It's 'the sign' and it's this sign that you will recognize, on your own time, in our family, the one who will take over from you when the moment comes."

He told Maria that nuns would claim he performed miracles and was a saint, but that he saw himself as merely a priest and "sorcerer," and he told Maria that she was a sorcerer as well.

"Don't be afraid. A sorcerer is not necessarily an evil being. They only become that if they want to, if they want to channel all their might towards evil. . . . And precisely because these powers, which I have, which you have, come from God, we must use them for good, to help others, to comfort those who have nothing." He warned her that this wouldn't be easy, and that she would have to make "heart-breaking" choices along the way, and that she may be even be forced to risk her own life.

After that, he began to wheeze, closing his eyes but continuing to speak. He said he could tell that Maria was scared of her own powers and the visions that took hold of her. The two of them continued to talk throughout the night, pausing only when interrupted by the occasional visit from a nurse. When the end was near, Maria opened the window so that her uncle could see his final sunrise. After he took his last breath, she ran out of the room and burst into tears.

This fantastical story echoed the one Maria had told in her letters, in which she said that her powers had been passed down to her by her uncle, who had been a beloved priest in a small Italian village. We didn't know what to think, but Françoise was clearly convinced by these stories.

She also told us a little about what it was like to work for the renowned psychic. "She was very demanding, very demanding," the former mayor said. "For example, if the phone rang, I shouldn't wait

for it to ring again. Two rings was the maximum. She was so percep-
tive, she needed everything to be exact. She never forgot anything,
she was extremely organized."

She said she didn't see Maria very often anymore, that her health
was deteriorating and that she no longer gave psychic consultations.
She did, however, confirm that Maria still lived in Callas and that she
was a local celebrity, but she stressed that Maria was very private.
Interestingly, she also confirmed that much of the detailed information in Maria's Wikipedia entry, which we'd originally dismissed,
was actually correct, including the fact that she had a son named
Antoine Palfroy.

There was one key piece of information that Wikipedia had wrong.

. . .

In our conversations with Françoise, she would make one small clari-
fication that led us to a massive discovery: Maria's real name was
Maria Carolina, but her last name was "Gamba," not "Gambia,"
which we'd seen on Wikipedia and in other online postings.

This was huge. We had struggled for months to find any truly
personal details about this woman. Searching the new spelling online brought us to a whole new trove of information—and most important, business filings with Maria's real name all over them.

These new documents were all written in French. We struggled
to make sense of all the legalese but were at least able to learn that
Maria really had been born in Milan, and that she'd become a French
citizen. The documents also gave us her birthdate, July 15, 1937,
meaning she was nearing her eightieth birthday.

These documents contained more than basic biographical details, though. Astroforce, the main company that had sent out the
Maria Duval letters for many years, appeared on them over and over

again. A French attorney helped interpret the filings and told us that the documents seemed to have been filed by a corporation named L'Estagnol, the same name we'd seen in the address for Maria listed on trademark filings. The value of her home was also listed, showing that it was appraised for around €762,000. We didn't know how old the appraisal was, but this suggested the home could be worth at least $1 million in US dollars today. So how did she get all this money? The filings provided a clue.

To our amazement, the French attorney told us that the documents showed that Maria had been the sole shareholder of the Swiss version of Astroforce. This is essentially what we'd seen on Wikipedia all those months ago, when we didn't even believe she was a real person. We knew that Astroforce had once been behind the letters, and the French filings also revealed that Maria had received nearly 207,000 Swiss francs (or around $200,000 in 2008 dollars) from the liquidation of the company in 2008—the same month of the French article heralding her return to Callas.

Finally, here it was, the proof we were looking for. Just as we had suspected, the same woman whose face was on all those letters had clearly profited from them. The only question was how much. If she had received similar payments in other years, then she could have easily made millions from this worldwide scam.

Armed with this new information, we were more ready than ever to try to confront Maria. We were also becoming increasingly nervous about whether we would be able to find her or get any answers to our questions. In preparation for our trip, we tried to get in touch with what appeared to be her only son, Antoine. We even sent messages to his wife and children. We were careful not to give away our upcoming travels, in case Antoine or Maria disappeared before we arrived. After all this, we couldn't come home empty handed.

As the days went on, Maria Duval became practically all we could think about. She haunted our thoughts and our dreams. Were we crazy to be flying all the way to France in search of an elderly psychic?

The Trip

Tᴇxᴛ ᴍᴇssᴀɢᴇ:

> Saturday, Jan. 23, 11:45 a.m.
> Melanie: Holy crap check your email
> Antoine emailed me

Antoine's email, which we quickly translated into English, landed in our inbox just hours before we set off on our trip.

> Hello,
> I am the son of Mrs. Maria Duval. You tried to contact me several times. My mother does not want to get in touch with you unless it's through her lawyer.
> I would ask you in the future to stop contacting my wife or children. Contact me but do not involve my family anymore.
> I'd appreciate if you told me what you want from me.
> Cordially,
> Antoine PALFROY

The timing couldn't have been worse, as we were planning to knock on her door as soon as we arrived in Callas. We were thrilled to have made contact with him—Maria's very own son—but we worried that we had gotten off on the wrong foot by bothering his wife and adult children, who we thought might lead us to him or his mother. Antoine's stern warning to leave Maria alone surely gave us second thoughts.

This was just the beginning of the day's drama. As we wrestled with Antoine's email, we grew increasingly concerned that we were going to arrive in France unable to speak with anyone around us—not to mention with Maria. Julia Jones, the French-speaking colleague who'd made the last round of phone calls for us, was scheduled to meet us in Callas. Much to our dismay, she lost her green card the day before our scheduled departure. We worried that she wouldn't be able to leave the United States without it. At the same time, a massive winter storm was brewing across the East Coast, which threatened to throw a wrench into her travel plans even if she was allowed to get past airport security. Without Julia, our expensive trek to France could all be in vain.

Then we began to worry about the two of us being able to make it there, especially since we were both coming from different cities. If we'd been able to watch the day unfold on a movie screen, the dramatic narration may have gone something like this.

Of the two intrepid female reporters, Blake had always been the free spirit. So while type A Melanie sat at her gate hours in advance, Blake wasn't quite as prepared. Thanks to unusually long security lines stretching around the Denver airport, as travelers from across the country were being rerouted because of the storm, she began her journey by missing her flight to Chicago, where she had been set to rendezvous with Melanie before the long red-eye flight to London. Melanie was already in the air as Blake pleaded with the gate agents to let her on her plane, which was still sitting on the runway. When Melanie landed and turned her phone on, she received a rapid-fire series of frantic text messages and emails from Blake alerting her that she'd missed her flight and would be flying straight to London. Melanie's stomach sank. She was already becoming increasingly nervous about the whole adventure, and she had been looking forward to seeing Blake, to hopefully put her own nerves at ease. Now, as she ate her cold airport falafel before boarding the dreaded plane, she wished she could just turn around and head back to sunny Los Angeles.

About eight hours later, Melanie landed in London, with just a few hours remaining before the short flight to Nice. Still there was no word from Blake. Worried that Blake had been waylaid yet again and not wanting to enter international security and risk leaving for Nice without her, Melanie paced back and forth in front of the winding lines, much to the chagrin of the airport employees, who kept telling her she was going to miss her flight. Finally, mere minutes before Melanie was about to give up and head to the gate alone, a panicked Blake came running full speed around the corner—attracting the attention of most people in the busy Heathrow terminal.

The two journalists barely had time to say hello to each other before the employees ushered them into the line. They were almost through the security checkpoint when Blake was pulled because she'd forgotten to remove her toiletries from her luggage. Instead of requiring her to remove them and try again, the security worker seemed to take pride in going as slowly as possible, looking carefully through every single one of Blake's items—as Melanie looked on in sheer terror.

Finally, after what felt like an eternity, Blake was cleared and the two of them sprinted to the gate, boarding the flight to Nice just in time. They settled into their uncomfortable airplane seats and breathed a sigh of relief. The worst was over.

. . .

A few short hours later, we landed in the beautiful city of Nice, ready for our hour-long drive to the hotel.

We could see the bright blue ocean as our plane landed, and after navigating through all the French signs in the airport, we made it to the rental car desk. Luckily the agent spoke English and told us he had one of the best vehicles for us. At our designated spot in the garage was a giant black Peugeot SUV. Our rental cars on past reporting trips had typically been cramped sedans, so we were impressed that we'd managed to score this vehicle with our modest budget for the trip.

As soon as we got on the road, we figured out why.

As tiny cars whizzed past us, our own vehicle was barely able to fit in the lanes of the main street leaving the airport. And as the roads got narrower on the way out of the city, we began to worry that we would hit cars trying to pass us or sideswipe parked vehicles and the large concrete walls bordering the right side of the road.

The drive started out easy enough despite the size of our car, all the signs in French, the endless roundabouts, and a dashboard that showed us our speed only in kilometers. But then our GPS began navigating us through winding mountain roads. At first we were in awe of the beautiful views around us. Soon, though, the sky got darker and darker and the hills got steeper and steeper, making the drive increasingly treacherous.

In retrospect, we can't help but laugh about what this must have looked like. Two American women driving alongside French cliffs at a snail's pace in a gigantic SUV that took up almost the entire narrow road. But at the time, it was terrifying. It was pitch-black outside, and every time we took a corner, we were afraid we would hit another car straight on.

We had no idea how fast we were going. It felt like we were flying until we noticed a line of cars piling up behind us. (We would later convert our speed of 60 kilometers an hour and realize we were moving along at less than 40 miles per hour.) On multiple occasions we tried to look for a place to pull over to let the other cars pass, if for nothing else but to get their bright lights out of our rearview mirror. With nowhere large enough to fit our car, though, we just kept going.

Those three hours of driving felt like days. Finally we pulled into Draguignan, a town neighboring Callas, where we had been able to find an affordable hotel at the last minute. There we met Julia, who we were so relieved had made it to France, and Jordan Malter, a producer from our video team who was there to document our search. Wearing the same clothes from the past thirty-six hours and looking especially shell-shocked after our harrowing drive, we greeted Julia in the hotel lobby to head to a much-needed dinner. Unlike us, she actually looked like she belonged in the South of France. Wearing a chic peacoat and black heels with her dark brown hair in a stylish bob, Julia looked ready for a night on the town. We just wanted a bottle of wine.

As we scarfed down some pizza at a nearby café, one of the only places open on a Sunday evening, we recounted our hellish journey to Julia and Jordan in painful detail. Rather than commiserate with us, they looked at each other in confusion, saying the drive they'd taken on the large French highway had been pretty simple. "Didn't you guys go through any tolls?" Julia asked.

That's when it hit us. As we had tried to figure out how to switch our French-speaking GPS to English, we'd selected the "no tolls" option, thinking French tollbooths would make an already foreign drive even more confusing.

Instead, we'd almost killed ourselves before we even got to Callas.

The Dusty Archives

THE NEXT MORNING we got up early, eager to leave our twin beds in our cold and sparsely furnished hotel room. We met Julia for a quick French breakfast of soft cheese, baguettes, and strong espresso as Julia told us that she had set up a meeting for us all the way back where we started the day before: Nice. The quick, easy trip on the French toll road made us especially embarrassed about the trek we had endured.

We were eager to try to confront Maria, but first wanted to gather as much information about her as we could. If she was once as popular as some of the reports claimed, the local newspaper should have proof. So we started our search in the dusty archives of *Nice-Matin*.

We were greeted by Alain, a tall and lanky man with thinning white hair. He was the paper's archivist, whose job it was to store and maintain the newspaper's decades of materials, including a digital archive in which he found several articles for us that mentioned Maria. He seemed thrilled that people actually needed his services and were interested in the dusty collection of documents he had spent so many years cultivating.

After struggling with his dated microfilm machine, he was finally able to pull up a newspaper article from 1992 that showed a picture of the psychic. "Maria Duval, voilà!" Alain exclaimed as he noticed her picture quickly scroll by on the screen. When it came into focus, we saw a much younger Maria standing next to what appeared to be a goose or a duck. After a quick skim of the article, Alain told us it said that Maria had returned to Callas from Paris that year because of her love of animals. "A witch, a gentle witch," he translated from the headline.

As we looked over his shoulder, he told us how he remembered Maria as a local celebrity for many years and that he had heard her on local radio stations giving horoscopes. He said he believed she was indeed a real psychic, saying it as matter-of-factly as you would say someone was a doctor or lawyer. We fired off question after question. Alain was happy to help but seemed confused about why we were so skeptical of this woman.

He was also eager to show us the newspaper's physical archives in a giant basement stuffed with bound books full of old newspapers. To get there, we packed ourselves into a metal freight elevator with flickering fluorescent lights and headed underground. After a short walk through a hallway that seemed to house forgotten furniture and other junk, we came upon a darkened room where we were immediately hit with the musty smell of old paper.

We had hoped that the newspaper's digital database would have been able to point us to any old articles about the psychic that might have been down there. But the database didn't go back far enough. We were stuck with trying to find them within a massive collection of hundreds of books, each of which contained hundreds of pages of newspaper. Luckily, we'd come with a few dates in mind, which helped us somewhat narrow our search. In our early reporting, we'd seen what appeared to be old newspaper clippings dug up by one of Maria's defenders and posted online. We'd assumed at the time that they were fake. Now we hoped to confirm our suspicions by going directly to the source.

The first article we were convinced was photoshopped featured large type suggesting that Maria had found someone by helicopter in Saint-Tropez—an eerily similar story to the one from her website and YouTube videos uploaded by gd2use. We showed the faded old clipping to Alain, but it didn't have a specific date to help guide his search, and he was unable to find it anywhere.

We looked for a different article, but the book that would have housed it was oddly missing from the shelf.

Moving on to the last one, Alain climbed up on his ladder and at one point looked like he was about to fall backward as he dragged the large, heavy book off the shelf. He proceeded to lay it down on the floor so we could all huddle around. "Where is it?" he said as we leafed through it until we got to the date we were looking for: September 25, 1977. Suddenly, in the bottom left-hand corner, we spotted a photo of a woman. Even though she had brown hair instead of her signature blond bob, it was definitely her. It was the exact same clipping that appeared online that we had thought was fake. Alain was as excited as we were, and he quickly gave us a rough translation of the small box of text beneath the photo.

"It says, somebody lost. And the family gave to this woman Maria Duval just a photo of the man who had been lost in the forest."

"Just looking at the photo," he said as he acted out the scene with his own palm in front of his wiry spectacles, "she was able to find this person. She is, how do you say in English when somebody has a sixth sense, somebody has a power?"

The Psychic No One Sees

MARIA WAS EVEN a mystery in the tiny town of Callas, where narrow cobblestone streets and country roads curved among vineyards and medieval buildings.

When we showed up in the center of Callas to look for any clues about Maria's real life, we were some of the only people around. Even in the summer months, the quaint town is far less of a tourist destination than the nearby port cities like Nice and Marseilles. In January, it was deserted. We parked next to the historic stone fountain and decided to pop our heads into any stores that were open.

Sitting at her desk in the small one-room tourism office on the way into town, a younger woman immediately recognized Maria's name. She described her as a well-known resident of Callas who wasn't in town much. She recalled having seen her at some local music festivals. And according to this woman, we were the first people she knew of who had come looking for Maria.

At a small, dimly lit restaurant that appeared to be one of the nicest in town, the middle-aged husband-and-wife owners weren't exactly excited to talk to us. Eventually we convinced the man to answer a few questions as his wife glowered at us disapprovingly.

"Personally, I don't know her. Physically, I've never seen her," the man told us. "She's lived here a while. But she's discreet."

Then there was the young clerk working the register at the tiny grocery store where we purchased a fresh baguette and a huge chunk of delicious French cheese for only a few euros. The worker, wearing glasses and a black puffy coat with a large hood, didn't even recognize the name. He said he had lived in the town his whole life and had worked in the store for a decade, but he had never heard of Maria.

We took our bread and cheese next door to a bar and tobacco shop, where a man wearing a tight black turtleneck served us tiny glasses of red wine in between ringing up packs of cigarettes and gum. As we devoured our food at an outside table, we were joined by a ruddy-faced, balding local man we'd met earlier by the fountain, who seemed very amused by us, as well as a little drunk, and who claimed to have the day off from work. He introduced himself as François.

He and Julia began speaking French to each other, while we tried to be involved in the conversation as much as we could, smiling and nodding along, picking up words here and there like *voyante* and "Duval" from within the conversation.

Soon François was joined by his friend Agostino, a round Italian man with gray hair and big black eyebrows. We showed them both a picture of Maria. Immediately they recognized her. "She's well known," François said. "But us, in a village like Callas, we're very down-to-earth. It's the winery, the olive trees, and that's it. We don't give a damn about psychics. She's more for the people abroad than here."

François said he had seen her around town a couple of times. It was Agostino, though, who had the most personal connection to her. He said he was one of the landscapers who had built her pool. "She's not an unpleasant person, but she's very . . . how can I say? She thinks of herself as very important, when she's not," he explained.

Just down the street, "Dame Jeanne," the owner of the town's only wine shop, was thrilled when we approached with a video camera. A tall, theatrical woman with short reddish-brown hair whose head almost reached the stone ceiling above her, she chatted with us in French from inside a dark and musty cave filled with bottles of French wine, gourmet spices, and other knickknacks. She knew who Maria was right away.

"She lives in the outskirts and I don't think she even buys her bread here," she told us.

"What do people say about her?" we asked.

"They don't."

"No?"

"No, honestly, no. You can ask any other shop owners here, no one knows her."

"Do you believe she's a psychic?"

"Me, I believe what I see. Maybe, but maybe it's also a good business model, huh? But me, I'm a very grounded person, so I have trouble [believing that]. I've never consulted with her."

"Do you know anyone who has consulted with her?"

"No."

"I think she is better known abroad than here," she added. "We don't go see psychics."

This seemed odd, considering what Maria's friend Françoise Barre, the former mayor, had claimed: that Maria's services were praised so highly.

Dame Jeanne seemed increasingly intrigued by our questions, asking whether we had met Maria. When we told her we had not, she explained that the only time she had ever seen her was at a pharmacy in a different town. "She's very proud," Dame Jeanne told us. "She had sent lists and lists of things she wanted from the pharmacist, Jean-Pierre, via fax, and by the time he got the fax, she was there, waiting in her Mercedes for her medication."

But in the seventeen years Dame Jeanne had owned her wine cave, she claimed to have never seen Maria in her store or anywhere else in Callas.

"She is the psychic that no one ever sees."

The House

WALLED IN BY giant slabs of impenetrable white concrete and a tall metal gate that towered above us, Maria Duval's house was clearly the home of someone who didn't want to be found.

Finding the place was an hours-long adventure in itself. We had two addresses for Maria, one from the nice woman who worked for the city of Callas and another from the public trademark applications. Our GPS didn't recognize either of them. So we typed in the two addresses over and over, attempting to find any version that the machine would recognize, and drove wherever it took us.

We started with the one from the town employee, which took us to the side of a cliff. At the end of a steep driveway was a sprawling estate. We knocked on the door but no one answered, and then we heard voices—but we couldn't tell where they were coming from. Worried that whoever was there might think we were trespassing, Julia called out *"Allo!" "Allo?"* in as friendly a voice as she could. Soon we saw two women walking toward us from the bottom of a tree-lined hill, and we squinted to see if either of them was elderly with blond hair. They were friendly enough, considering we were strangers standing on their property, but neither of them was Maria, nor could they tell us where to find her.

We returned to our car and typed in the second address, "L'Estagnol, Les 4 chemins," the same address listed on many of Maria's public trademark documents. It was located miles away from the estate, and to get there we'd have to travel through more winding mountain roads. When we drove up to a four-way stop, our GPS announced that we had arrived at our destination. We pulled over to the side of the road, but we couldn't find any houses. We looked at Google Maps on our phones, which showed that the intersection had a name, Les quatre chemins, which roughly translates to "the four paths."

The hours passed and soon it would be dark. We still had no idea where Maria Duval lived. Confronting her had been the whole goal of our trip. Dejected, we decided to go back to the hotel to strategize. Driving away, something caught our eye: a faded yellow sign with "L'Estagnol!" written on it in cursive. It sat outside a run-down stucco home with white shutters and a red tiled roof. This was when we realized that the trademark address had taken us to the right place, but we didn't have a house number. We looked back at the number of the other address, thinking that it might correspond to the address for her house. It didn't match the house in front of us but suggested it was just down the road. We must have driven right past it.

We flipped a U-turn and parked on a little dirt path next to a large horse stable and riding area, convinced her house must be within walking distance.

Almost directly across the street, we saw the number we had been looking for on what appeared to be a laminated piece of paper, nailed into the trunk of a large tree. Next to the tree was a metal gate chained shut with a silver padlock, connected to a beat-up chain-link fence that spanned the entire front of the property. We couldn't see a house, only an overgrown dirt road surrounded by trees, fallen leaves, and brush. On the gate, an old red sign warned that this was private property. Nearby was another sign that contained an image of the head of a dog, which warned that visitors entered at their own peril. Above the gate there was a yellow sign stating that the property was under twenty-four-hour surveillance. When we looked up, a security camera was pointed right at us. If there was some sort of house down this road and Maria Duval were there, we were convinced that we were not going to get to her.

We continued to walk along the side of the street, crunching piles of dead leaves with our boots and passing speeding cars as we followed the chain-link fence and walked past more of the same yellow surveillance signs. It felt like we were in the middle of nowhere until the occasional car came rushing by on the main road, reminding us we weren't alone.

A few hundred feet down the side of the road a house appeared.

It was clearly two stories tall and white, but a large white wall and a looming metal gate—with two concrete eagles perched atop each side—kept us from seeing anything more. We were able to get a glimpse of the roof from the road; the house wasn't far behind the gate, but the thick greenery planted all around it kept the property hidden from anyone passing by. There was a sign that said "Beware of Dog" in French, on which someone had used a marker to change the word "Dog" to "Dogs."

And there was a buzzer.

Uneasy, we pushed the white button.

Silence.

We waited a minute and buzzed again.

And again.

Slowly, the gate began to creep open.

It felt as if everything was moving in slow motion. Gradually, the solid white metal panels began to part, revealing glimmers of a woman standing only feet away.

After all this time and speculation, were we finally going to meet the woman herself?

Then, just as abruptly as it had opened, the gate stopped moving, leaving only a narrow opening between the two thick panels.

Julia quickly tried to get the attention of whoever was back there. *"Allo?" "Bonjour?"*

Then she locked eyes with a blond woman and the gate began to reverse course—closing with a clang amid the sound of angry, barking dogs. Worried that we'd lost our chance, Julia quickly began speaking to whoever this was—as the two of us stood by panicked and helpless.

> JULIA: *I'm looking for Madame Maria Duval.*
> THE WOMAN: *No. She's not here at the moment. What do you want?*
> JULIA: *We're journalists and we have questions for her.*
> THE WOMAN: *Madame Duval is in Rome at the moment.*

Out of the conversation between Julia and the woman, we were able to make out that this was indeed the home of Maria Duval. The woman, who claimed she worked for Maria, told us to leave a note for the psychic in the mailbox next to us. As the conversation continued, we noticed a large, brown snout that appeared to belong to a Rottweiler emerge from under the spikes of a side gate. The dog looked straight at us with big, dark eyes that made it clear we weren't welcome.

The woman proceeded to tell us that she couldn't open the gate because of the dogs, and that she needed to go.

JULIA: *OK, what's your name, madame?*
(Silence.)
JULIA: *Just to know who I spoke to?*
(Silence.)
JULIA: *Hello? Madame? Madame?*

She was gone, her black shoes silently disappearing from under the gate.

All that was left was the growling dog.

As soon as we were absolutely sure she had left, we turned to Julia, the only one who'd gotten a good look at the woman. "Was it Maria?" we whispered into the cold winter air.

Unfortunately, Julia was convinced that the woman couldn't possibly have been Maria. While the woman behind the gate did indeed have blond hair, Julia told us that the person she'd seen was much too young to be the elderly psychic from the letters.

Maybe the real Maria was hiding inside. It seemed far too convenient that she'd taken a quick vacation to Rome the very same week we'd flown all the way to France to try to meet her. Either way, we followed the woman's instructions and scribbled a letter to Maria on a page ripped from one of our notebooks. With the sun setting against a darkening sky, we walked back across the street, our feet again crunching the dead leaves beneath them, and placed the note in Maria's small white mailbox.

Hello, Ms. Duval,

We're journalists from CNN in the United States. We are currently writing an article about you and the letters sent in your name around the world, and we'd like to give you an opportunity to share your perspective on the story.

Please contact us as soon as possible, since it's very important that we speak to you—and if at all possible, in person.

Sincerely,
Melanie Hicken,
Blake Ellis

The Sister

W E WOKE UP the next morning still on a mission to somehow get to Maria.

We piled into Julia's hotel room to strategize after another quick breakfast of espresso, bread, and cheese. While the two of us were relegated to a dark box of a room, which contained little more than two beds, Julia's room was drenched with sunlight and had views of charming red rooftops nearby. It also had a desk and several chairs, all of which made it a much more conducive space for our sleuthing.

We quickly dumped out our file folder full of the documents we'd brought along on our trip, and spread them over Julia's queen-size bed. Looking for any last clues, we returned to the personal business filings for Maria Gamba Duval that we'd discovered shortly before leaving for France. We'd been in such a hurry during our initial review of these documents that this time we noticed a new name: Marie-Françoise Gamba.

Wondering who this woman could be (and guessing it must be a fake name or a relative of Maria's), we turned to our laptops and were surprised to quickly find a French phone listing online. Our marathon calling sessions to date had resulted in so many dial tones that we were even more surprised when an elderly sounding, French-speaking woman picked up the phone soon after Julia punched in the number.

Julia, also startled, quickly put the woman on her speakerphone, as the two of us anxiously stood over her shoulder listening. Julia introduced herself as a journalist and asked about her connection to Maria. Upon hearing her response, Julia looked up at us with big eyes and muted the line.

It was Maria Duval's sister, Julia whispered.

Again, and this time more than ever, we desperately wished we could understand every word this woman was saying. We did recognize a few words, though, the most important of which were "Switzerland," "Jacques," "letters," and "Infogest."

Getting more and more excited, we started shoving notes and questions in front of Julia, scribbled on the back of the very business filings that had given us this woman's name. When we eventually returned to these filings months later, we were amused by the crumpled pages full of hastily written questions. But at the time, Julia took page after page from us, asking each question of Maria's sister in succession.

"Do you talk to your sister often?"

"Is your sister still involved with any businesses?"

"Where did your sister get all her money?"

"Tell your sister there are *still* letters being sent out in her name."

Julia, who we were quickly learning was a master multitasker, jotted down her own notes and responses as she spoke with Marie-Françoise. When she hung up the phone, we were champing at the bit for a full recap of the conversation. Maria's sister had provided us with another small breakthrough.

She'd told Julia that she spoke with her sister almost every day, and that Maria was not in good health. She hadn't said whether her condition was the result of some kind of sickness or simply old age. Also, she'd seemed shocked when Julia explained that the US government had filed a lawsuit against Maria alleging mail fraud. After hearing a description of the letters and the money they asked for, Maria's sister called it an "escro" (short for *escroquerie*), a French word for "scam." "There's no way my sister created the letters," she told Julia.

She had a possible explanation for everything that we hadn't heard before, though: She said that many years ago, Maria had sold the rights to her name to a Swiss company, which her sister thought was likely Infogest, and that Maria didn't have anything to do with what happened afterward. Although she didn't remember names of specific businessmen, her sister told us that Maria "was involved with a Jacques."

What Maria's sister told us about this business deal seemed plausible. What seemed less believable was the idea that Maria, given the YouTube videos and media interviews in which she publicly acknowledged and defended the letters, had absolutely nothing to do with them.

Soon after our call with Maria's sister, we called back Maria's close friend Françoise Barre, the former mayor of Callas whom we'd spoken to weeks earlier. She still wouldn't meet us in person but agreed to speak with us over the phone. "She had her company that took care of her," she told us, suggesting that a business arrangement had been made to oversee the letters and the money they brought in.

When Julia told her that the letters were being used to deceive people, she actually didn't seem surprised. "Yes it's possible," she said. "Yes, yes, she told me a long time ago, 'I no longer have control over them.'"

On a more personal note, she again stressed to us that Maria was a good person, calling her "loyal and competent." She was unwavering about her psychic abilities. "She has an extraordinary power for divination to predict the future," the former mayor asserted. "She told me, 'You will be mayor.'"

Now in possession of this additional evidence tying the psychic to the scam, we were even more eager to speak with Maria. Her sister, before our call ended, told us something that made it seem like it might be worth another try.

She said that, given Maria's health, she would be very surprised if the psychic was actually in Rome. And she would know, we figured. After all, she claimed to speak with her sister almost every day.

The Pot of Jelly

W E WERE HESITANT to return to Maria's house a second time. Still fresh in our minds was the email from Maria's son, Antoine, warning us to stay away from his mother.

We pulled up to her property and parked in the same spot as before, next to the same large stable. We were still in the car, discussing our game plan, when we suddenly noticed that her gate was opening, and a large white van was beginning to pull out from the entrance. Determined not to lose our chance, we swung open our car doors and sprinted across the street without even grabbing our notebooks.

As the van turned out of the driveway and began down the main road, we frantically flagged down the startled driver. An older man cautiously rolled down the window, likely curious to know what three young women and a man with a video camera could possibly want from him. When we asked him about Maria, he said he was her gardener, and that she was in Rome and he didn't know when she would be returning. "I don't know about her business, and she doesn't want us to," he said.

Before we could ask him any more of our questions, other cars started to approach behind him on the one-lane road, and he quickly pulled away—leaving us standing there alone.

With nothing to lose, we left the middle of the road and continued to the gate again.

If Maria really wasn't in Rome, as her sister suspected, then this was a pretty well-orchestrated cover-up, with even her gardener being told the same story—or at least told to tell it to anyone who came knocking. But how would Maria have known we were coming? Antoine was the only one besides her sister who knew we were in France. Could he have tipped her off?

We were convinced Maria had to be in that house. We walked the perimeter of the property trying to spot a light on in one of the rooms or a face looking out at us from a window. We craned our necks, jumped as high as we could to try to see over the fence and the large concrete wall. We held our phones above our heads attempting to take zoomed-in photos with our cameras. Still, we still saw nothing.

So we returned to the main gate and tried the same buzzer from the day before, pushing it again and again. This time there was no answer.

• • •

Fresh off the futile effort to find Maria at her home, we returned to Callas's town hall the following day, to see if the friendly woman who'd given us Maria's address might have more to share.

We took the quick drive from our hotel and parked at the bottom of a hill that led into town. We then walked through narrow alleys dotted with flowers and ornate doors and shutters as we followed the small wooden signs for *Maire* (mayor) before eventually reaching the town hall, which was tucked away at the top of a steep cobblestone street overlooking the rolling hills and vineyards of Callas.

It was a busy day inside, with only two people manning the front desk. We sat across from a painted mural of the town, trying to read the various flyers and brochures advertising senior fitness classes and other local events as we waited to be seen. When we were eventually called in, we were greeted by a different woman than the one we had spoken with on the phone. This middle-aged blond lady said she had actually worked for Maria more than twenty years earlier. As an intern.

Thinking about our own college internships at newspapers and magazines, we thought that working for a psychic seemed very odd, so we were dying to hear more about this unique apprenticeship. Unfortunately, she wouldn't go into much detail about what she actually did for Maria as an intern. She explained that she worked at Maria's house, the same one we had tried to visit, and that she was unaware of any complaints against her.

Of course, she wasn't the first person we'd talked to who had worked for Maria. The former mayor said she had been the psychic's personal secretary for many years, the same title Jacques Mailland had used to describe his relationship with her as well. And there was a man referred to as her business manager in the local newspaper article heralding her retirement. For a small-town psychic, she had gathered quite the army of people around her.

When we asked this town hall worker about the last time she'd seen the psychic, she told us one of the most confusing things we had heard thus far. Quite casually, she said that Maria actually came by the town hall around the holidays to pick up a pot of coulis. Since coulis is a pureed fruit or vegetable sauce similar to jelly, we thought we must have lost something in translation when Julia relayed the conversation to us. Could a single pot of jelly really be enough to convince a reclusive celebrity to venture into town?

Julia asked the woman if she was understanding her correctly. Yes, the woman explained. As part of a senior citizen program, every resident over the age of sixty was given a pot of coulis at the end of the year. They just had to come into the office to collect it.

The Lover

THIS WAS AN interesting—and amusing—development. But it didn't get us any closer to figuring out where Maria was these days.

We still couldn't find anyone in Callas who had seen her since her jelly pickup in December. Her friend the former mayor also hadn't seen her in a while, nor had Maria's sister. It seemed especially strange when Maria's neighbors, whom we tried talking to after accosting her gardener in the middle of the street, didn't seem to even know who she was, let alone if she was home.

Increasingly desperate, we set our sights on the man who had been named as her business manager in the local newspaper article. At the time, we hadn't thought much of it. But as we ran out of other options, we became determined to find this man. Our online research showed that he owned a business nearby and provided us with an address that took us to the middle of an industrial park that reeked of sulfur.

We knew this man had some sort of business in this center but didn't know where it was. There were rows of buildings in the complex, and since most were empty, we were excited to see a glimpse of people inside one of them. It ended up being a packed yoga class, and when we barged in and interrupted it the instructor wasn't even fazed, telling us the business we were looking for was around the corner, all while shouting out new poses to her class of older women.

She was right. Around the corner and just down the road was a home construction business. A friendly younger man watched us through the window as we walked in the door, and he was surprisingly forthcoming. He told us that the man had indeed been Maria's manager, but that there was more to their relationship than that. They had been involved in a romantic affair for many years, he said, but the manager was a married man, and he had left Maria in 2009 (the year after the article we'd found had been published), ending their relationship.

He then handed us a bright yellow Post-it note containing this man's personal phone number, which we called as soon as we piled back into the car. When we got him on the phone, he wasn't happy to share any personal details. Speaking to us in a loud, gruff voice, he was adamant that he had never had any personal relationship with Maria, telling us he worked at her house for only a month as a construction manager and hadn't spoken to her in ten years. We asked him why Maria would have lied about him being her business manager. He said she was an important person at the time and probably thought it would make her sound more official if she had a manager. This sounded like something she would do, he added bitterly.

He said he knew nothing about the Maria Duval letters, and that he had been outraged when he'd seen his name in that article listed as her manager. He told us that he'd called the newspaper to demand a correction.

After our call, we remembered that Alain, the chatty archivist, had printed out all the most recent articles about Maria for us. We quickly flipped through the printouts and found the article in which the business manager was listed. Placed at the bottom of it, there was a correction noting that this man was "no longer the manager for the astrologer and clairvoyant Maria Duval."

The Son

W E HAD SEVERAL days left in France and were at a complete loss of what to do next. Part of us wanted to scrap the whole endeavor, happy to spend the rest of our time in the South of France tasting wine at all the beautiful vineyards we kept passing.

We had spoken with everyone from Maria Duval's gardener to her alleged lover and business manager. We had gone to her house. We had hand-delivered a note to her mailbox. We had left multiple voice mails on her machine. We had even spoken with her sister. Nearly out of ideas for how to reach Maria, we turned back to our limited interactions with Antoine, Maria's son.

When we received that initial email from him on the way to the airport, we had quickly replied, asking him if he would be willing to speak with us and answer some questions about his mother and the letters. In response, he'd sent us a gruff message asking what we wanted to know. So we promptly sent him some questions and again asked to speak with him, but he didn't respond, even after multiple follow-ups.

Before leaving on our trip, we had created an extensive dossier on Antoine, complete with large photos of him and his family members, along with phone numbers that were listed for him. We called the numbers to no luck. Nearly out of options, we cautiously considered showing up at his doorstep.

. . .

We were both intrigued and concerned when our research on Maria's son showed that he was a member of the international secret society known as the Free and Accepted Masons, or Freemasons.

All we knew about Freemasonry was that it was a centuries-old international brotherhood shrouded in mystery that elicited images of intricate symbols and underground meetings. Researching this group took us on yet another detour. The United Grand Lodge of England, viewed by many as the organization's headquarters and the place where it all started, describes Freemasonry on its website as a "non-religious," "non-political" charity dating back to the 1700s or even earlier and boasts of famous past members including Winston Churchill, Buffalo Bill, and Harry Houdini.

> *Freemasonry is a society of men concerned with moral and spiritual values. Its members are taught its principles (moral lessons and self-knowledge) by a series of ritual dramas—a progression of allegorical two-part plays which are learnt by heart and performed within each Lodge—which follow ancient forms, and use stonemasons' customs and tools as allegorical guides. . . . Freemasonry instils in its members a moral and ethical approach to life: its values are based on integrity, kindness, honesty and fairness.*

Reading this noble mission statement on various Freemason websites, one wouldn't think the group was anything to be afraid of. Outside of the organization's own description, however, it was easy to find countless conspiracy theories about the suspected nefarious activities taking place behind the walls of this group's mysterious meeting lodges. These theories included wild claims that Freemasons were Satan worshippers, ritualistic murderers, or even part of the Illuminati—a notorious secret society associated with frightening conspiracy theories that made us think of a Dan Brown novel.

We also found an interesting article about Freemasonry and its reputation in France specifically. It appeared that this group was much more controversial in France than in the United States. "The way the French see it, Masons are a fifth column at the heart of French society, a cabal of powerful politicians, businessmen, and intellectuals with a hidden agenda that is difficult to pin down because it's, well, hidden. Nobody knows quite what the Masons are up to, but everybody suspects they're up to something," stated a Bloomberg News article headlined "France: Where Freemasons Are Still Feared."

Antoine seemed to be so involved with this community that he had even trademarked his own Masonic organization, which described itself as a spiritual, symbolic, philosophical, and occult group. The information on its website was very difficult for us to decipher— and not just because it was in French. "According to the traditional principles of the Order, the three Great Lights surround the Square, the Compass, the Rule and the Sacred Book which are on the Altar of Oaths, the Naos, in the center of the Lodge, a very strong place and very enlightened," it stated in one place, reminding us of some of the spiritual and psychic gibberish we'd read in Maria's letters and heard in her interviews.

He was involved in a number of other spiritual organizations as well. One described itself as a gathering of men and women "of Desire." Another was connected to a mystical order known as Martinism; and as we read more about it we were surprised to see a mention of psychic powers. "At the higher spiritual level you will benefit from improvement in awareness, as evidenced in intuitive flashes and special psychic abilities. The potential benefits are infinite," said the Martinist magazine, *Pantacle*. It went on to explain that Martinism is based on esoteric teachings, involving everything from alchemy to tarot cards.

We also knew that Antoine owned a bookstore named La table d'Hermès, which appeared to organize workshops on spirituality and sell tarot cards, Masonic memorabilia, and incense.

All of this felt a little eerie, yet it was another reason Antoine could be the key to finding out more about Maria.

· · ·

We couldn't wait to check out Antoine's eclectic bookstore for ourselves and hopefully find him in the process. As our luck would have it, after decades of operations, it had apparently just gone out of business. The bookstore's telephone number was disconnected, as Antoine's personal numbers had been. Neighboring store owners we called told us that the shop had closed six months earlier. But it was located in Toulon, only an hour away from our hotel. So we decided to drive there anyway—never expecting things would play out the way they did.

After spending what seemed like hours trying to fit our SUV into tiny parking spaces, we walked through the center of town, past *crêperies*, candy shops, and busy outdoor cafés on our way to Antoine's shop. While the town was relatively quiet on this January afternoon, we could easily picture it bustling with tourists during the summer, when it was a popular port for cruise ships.

We finally arrived at the little store, which sat right next to a charcuterie. It was dark, empty, and obviously out of business. We stared at the locked door and vacant shelves inside, and noticed a sign for a tarot card reader advertising hour-long consultations at the store for fifty euros each. We had already figured out that Antoine was a spiritual guy but were becoming more and more convinced that he was part of the local psychic community, like his mother.

Next to this ad was a for-sale sign with a phone number, which we guessed was for the real estate agent who was trying to sell the place. Out of other options, we tried the number to see if the broker could possibly put us in touch with Antoine.

Right there, standing outside his store, we called. It was Antoine himself who answered.

As Julia talked to him, we couldn't believe this last-ditch effort had somehow landed us on the phone with Maria Duval's son. He never admitted to avoiding our many, many attempts to reach him. He instead suggested we meet in person. He told us to come to a café called Le Chantilly near his now-defunct bookshop in Toulon two days later—the day before we were scheduled to leave Callas.

The Attorney

I N THE DAYS leading up to the big meeting with Antoine, there was one more person we wanted to find: Andrea Egger, the Swiss attorney who seemed to have been deeply involved with the Maria Duval operation and who we had been unsuccessfully trying to reach for months. This mission took us to one of the strangest and most beautiful places we had ever been: the tiny city-state of Monaco, where we had found an address for Andrea.

Both a luxurious waterfront getaway and a notorious tax haven, Monaco is wildly popular among high rollers, who frequent its five-star resorts and world-famous casinos. But it is also known to be an oasis for unscrupulous businessmen, who are drawn to the financial secrecy the location provides. Even from the window of our car, we wondered about the backstories of all those we passed, with their designer clothing and flashy watches. Where was all their money coming from?

While Andrea Egger wasn't named in any of the government actions we had seen, or been charged with any wrongdoing in connection with Maria Duval, he had filed a number of trademark applications for both Maria and many of the businesses associated with her name. His was one of the first names we'd heard in our months-long hunt, when the New York attorney told us he communicated with Andrea via airmail when securing Maria's very first US trademark. This attorney had described Andrea as a woman, but we'd since seen the name listed as a male on multiple Swiss business filings.

A bare-bones Facebook page featured a profile picture of a sandy-haired man shirtless on the beach. Another photo showed him reclining in a lounge chair reading a newspaper. He appeared to be in his sixties, and he had an attractive but unmemorable face. Between this and his LinkedIn profile, we read claims that he had attended school in Geneva, studied at Columbia Law School in New York City, and worked for a large investment bank. Despite his impressive résumé, we found little evidence of his legal work beyond his name being listed on so many different Maria Duval filings.

We had spent months trying to reach Andrea. Then, as we sat at our computer in our French hotel room looking through business filings once more, we spotted a personal address for him in Monaco. As it was only a couple hours away from our hotel, we knew we had to give it a shot.

The drive there was gorgeous, unlike anything we had seen before, taking us through rock tunnels that cut straight into the sides of seaside cliffs. We passed a few men sitting at the border for security, and the streets became narrower and narrower as we drove into the center of town. It was such a small city that it was easy to locate his address, which appeared to be a high-rise apartment building. The problem was finding somewhere to park our SUV.

Down the road sat a vacant garage attached to a luxurious building, which we thought was a hotel because of the many large flags hanging out front. It turned out to be a very private residential building, and as soon as we entered, the security guards discovered we were not residents and promptly escorted us to our car, with a man in uniform watching us to ensure we left the premises.

Back on the narrow streets, we drove in an upward spiral, trying to find anywhere to park. After a stressful drive that rivaled our treacherous trip that first day in France, we finally found a true public parking lot.

In our desperation, we'd driven so high up that we had to trek down flight after flight of stairs and take a public elevator to get from practically the highest point of the hillside town back down to shore level. Andrea lived in a circular luxury building that sat just along the water. Curious about what such a residence would cost someone, we later looked for listings and found a two-bedroom unit for rent for €13,000 a month and another for sale for €6 million. To afford such a pricey pad, Andrea must have been successful at something.

Finally it was time to confront this elusive man. Without a specific unit number, we walked into his building and headed straight past the security guard to the elevator, hoping there might be nameplates for the residents inside. We exited the elevator at a random floor and encountered nothing but barely lit hallways that felt like something out of a horror movie—and no names to be found. With no other options beyond aimless wandering through the dozens of floors in this large high-rise, we returned to the lobby and Julia buttered up the doorman with her singsongy French before asking him for the suite number. Knowing there was a very slim chance that this man would sacrifice the privacy of his tenant, we were elated when he gave us the precise apartment number and let us hop back in the elevator.

We made it onto the correct floor and used the flashlight on our phones to try to find Andrea's unit number. We walked briskly, running on a combination of adrenaline and fear, remembering that we were three young women (Jordan had returned to New York City the day before) in a strange building, in a strange land, looking for a man we were convinced was unscrupulous at best.

Eventually we found the door and looked at each other, wondering what to do next. If Andrea was in there, he clearly wouldn't be happy to see us, three CNN journalists who had been digging up information about him and raising questions about his role in a multimillion-dollar fraud.

If he had a knife or a gun, was there anything to keep him from using it as we stood very alone in this very dark hallway? People surely killed for less. Had we even told our bosses or our family where we were going? If we went missing, would anyone know where to find us?

Nevertheless, we couldn't leave without ringing his doorbell. Once, twice, and a third time.

No answer—something we were very much getting used to. This time, we had to admit, we were kind of glad to still be standing in silence. Still, as journalists it was our duty to make sure this man knew that we were writing our story and that he would be a part of it, and to see if he had anything to say for himself.

We walked over to a corner of the hallway so were out of sight of his door's peephole in case he was looking out at us, and we crouched down to write him a note on yet another piece of paper ripped from our reporter's notebook. We walked back and quickly slid the note under his door, before dashing to the elevator and getting out of the building as fast as we could. Julia did take a moment to ask the doorman if he had seen Mr. Egger lately, to which he said he hadn't.

We made it out of the building and back into the bright sunlight to breathe a sigh of relief. Slowly over the next few hours, our fear and panic were replaced with a satisfying picture of Andrea returning to his home to find a note slipped under his door—from three American journalists.

The Deal

PART OF US never thought Antoine was really going to show up to our scheduled meeting.

We had returned to our hotel in Draguignan after our excursion to Monaco, and the next day we drove to Toulon hours in advance to scout out the perfect spot for our late-afternoon interview. The airy two-story café Antoine had selected was adorned with glass chandeliers and detailed crown molding. We settled on a quiet nook upstairs with a tufted velvet couch and a small table and went over our questions at length, preparing ourselves for what was to come. We suspected Antoine didn't speak much English, so Julia was even more nervous, knowing she would bear the brunt of the interview.

Finally, the man from our dossier began walking over to our table. He had a round face, short graying hair, and wire-rimmed glasses. And his daughter was with him. We knew it was her because of the photo of a dark-featured young woman that we'd printed out from LinkedIn. We were right that he didn't feel comfortable speaking in English, so after shaking his hand and saying *"Bonjour,"* we awkwardly smiled and nodded our heads as he and Julia went through their formalities. While he was skeptical of our motives at first, even asking to see our official CNN IDs before he would say anything, the conversation ended up lasting for more than an hour. It could have gone much longer if we hadn't gotten kicked out by the barista when the café closed, which we were convinced had been Antoine's plan all along.

We started out with some biographical questions, asking about his mother's life and what she was like. Even though Julia was the only one who understood what he was saying, he looked each of us in the eye as he spoke. He began by telling us that after being born in Italy, Maria had come to France when she was young, and it was during this time in her life that she first realized her psychic gift. He said that there was no question his mother was a real psychic, and that she had started out intent on helping others. "As a little girl, things she would see would then happen," he said.

And even as her life took her in another direction, as she ran an industrial pool-cleaning business and opened four different clothing stores around the South of France, her psychic abilities remained, and she started giving psychic consultations to friends from her clothing stores. Eventually, as word of her powers spread, she began appearing on local television and radio, writing horoscopes and being called on by police and families to locate missing people.

This yet again made us wonder whether some of the outlandish stories from the letters could actually be based on something more than a copywriter's imagination, including the repeated claim that Maria had used her powers to locate the missing. Especially curious was the fact that Antoine even specifically mentioned the missing man from Saint-Tropez—the same story we'd heard Maria tell in her YouTube video, and very similar to the story involving the missing dentist's wife. And while we hadn't been able to locate an article about a Saint-Tropez rescue in the dusty archives of the local newspaper, the archivist had found one clipping that said Maria had helped find a missing elderly man. If she really had found so many missing people, it was interesting to us that he chose to mention the one she'd recounted in her promotional YouTube video.

We also asked about the so-called Callas Parapsychology Institute, which was mentioned in all the letters as well, and to our confusion Antoine said that Maria had indeed been the president of the association a long time ago. We were never able to find any evidence of this group, even after reaching out to the Parapsychological Association in France.

Antoine also claimed that his mother really had meet the pope, even shaken his hand, though he acknowledged it was from within a crowd of people and nothing like the personal consultation described in the letters.

He said she had been married multiple times, to his father and later to another man. Her second marriage hadn't lasted very long. We had suspected that Duval was nothing more than a stage name. Some investigators had referred to the name as an alias. But according to Antoine, it actually was the name she'd taken from her second husband.

"What's it like to grow up with a psychic as a mom?" we asked him at the beginning of our meeting.

"Dangerous," he answered. "You can't do anything stupid. It's delicate. . . . She'd say, 'How was your day?' and then ask, 'And what did you really do?'"

"She never used her gift in an obvious way," chimed in his daughter Morgane, who, unlike her grandmother, had dark hair and dark features. "It was always more subtle. She gave us advice in our professional choices, in our love lives."

"She gets up really early, five a.m., and stays up," Antoine added.

"She takes no vacations. She is very passionate about her work. She does a lot of astrology, she's always done it, since I was little."

Despite her old age and the sickness we'd heard about, Antoine said his mother remained eager to continue to help people, after years of advising everyone from politicians to employers and investors. "She has always been someone who loved to work with people, have conversations, she liked that very much," he said. "Meeting new people. She has worked with ministers, with regular people, that was never an issue. She loved helping people, talking to people."

When Julia later filled us in on this part of the conversation, we couldn't help but recall some of the stories Maria recounted in one of the YouTube videos. She claimed to have helped bank executives make financial decisions and crucial hires using her psychic abilities. Could there be an inkling of truth in those videos, which we had viewed as pure propaganda? Or maybe Antoine just knew exactly what to say.

We were most curious about how his mother had become wrapped up in the scam. The story that unfolded was the tale of a woman who'd made a deal with the devil.

"How did the letters start?" we asked.

"Well, these letters . . . my mother sold her name."

"Do you know when?"

"At least twenty years ago. And from the moment when the name was sold, the name didn't belong to my mother anymore . . . it belonged to a company that could do with it whatever it wanted."

"Do you know the name of the company?"

"No."

"Infogest?"

"Maybe. That rings a bell."

"Do you remember any names?"

"No, I cannot give you any names, that you'd have to see with my mother's lawyer, since there is a lawsuit."

We would ask him again and again after this to speak with this lawyer, but he never did give us a name.

"So we know she copyrighted her name in 1985, and this was before selling her name. Do you know why she did that?"

"To protect her name. She was already known under that name for a while. She started going by that in the seventies. . . . And since she helped find people who were lost. . . . Little by little she was known by that. Since it was in the newspapers, and she certainly had a real gift for clairvoyance."

We pressed him again. If her reputation was so important to her, then why did she sell her name?

"I think there was a big company that proposed a lot a money."

"They came to her?"

"It was the company that came to her, I think. Because she was well known. She practiced in Draguignan and Nice. She was on TV, on *Matin Bonheur* [a French morning show], then on newspapers. She also did television donation marathons. She even went to the US following the election of Reagan."

This was news to us. We had not seen any evidence of her being on US soil; nor did we find any after this interview.

"Did she ever send any letters?"

"No."

"So did she know what was being done with her name?"

"I'm not sure. I don't think so. She knew there were things going on, but whether she likes it or not, there's nothing she can do about it. The name was sold so she had no more decision power."

We were skeptical, asking him if she truly didn't know about the letters.

"Not really. It was all the companies. For example, she had to go to Russia, Japan, to show people that Maria Duval exists—that it's not just a name, there's a physical person."

"So it was for the companies that she traveled? She was paid?"

"Yes, but that was part of the contract. From the moment she is bound by the contract, she cannot do otherwise, whether she liked it or not."

"What was the last time she made an appearance?"

"About two or three years ago in Russia."

"Do they still ask her to do appearances?"

"I'm not sure, I think there have been problems, I can't tell you what problems."

"There are currently horoscopes with her name running in Russian newspapers. Is she making those predictions?"

"No, it's a company. She can't use her name. It's delicate. We can't stop this contract, or it's preferable not to."

"When she sold her name, did they explain the terms of the contract to her?"

"I don't think so. No, no, no."

We had heard, albeit in less detail, this same story earlier in the week, from Maria's sister and friend, and we were still struggling to wrap our heads around how someone could enter into a contract that would cede all control over how her very own name was used without understanding the risks or repercussions.

"Was she ever afraid of being involved in lawsuits relating to the letters?"

"Of course, but what could she do? She was very upset, and also with the way they used her name."

"Did she ever try to get out?"

He laughed. And from there, the conversation began to take a more sinister tone.

"It's not the kind of contract you get out of. It's better to not try to get out of it."

"Because she'd have to return money?"

"I don't know exactly."

As we pressed Antoine about this, why she was so afraid of getting out of her contracts, he became noticeably more uncomfortable and tight-lipped.

"Does she still receive any money?"

"I don't think she receives any more money, no."

"Because in the US lawsuit they mention $180 million," we said, referencing the bare minimum investigators said the scam raked in from victims in the United States.

"That'd be nice," he said, laughing. "You need to differentiate two things. Like I am Antoine Palfroy, that's my name. If I sell it, I am still Antoine Palfroy, but the name doesn't belong to me any longer, commercially. If tomorrow my mother wanted to open a store under the name Maria Duval, she couldn't. It's a brand. So if the company is making millions of dollars, that's not hers."

"Do you know how much she has received?"

"No, that I don't know."

"Just to clarify, she never wrote any of these letters?"

"No, of course not."

Right there was his answer to one of the biggest questions we had. Could it really be true that she had nothing to do with creating the content of these letters even though the whole scam depended on her personal story—a personal story that we'd discovered had a lot of truth to it? If Maria wasn't the one directly dictating the details of her life to include, maybe the copywriters had acquired all these personal details and anecdotes from newspaper articles. Or maybe they came straight from one of the businessmen who knew her personally, like Jacques Mailland.

"And what do you think of that?" we asked, still perplexed by the idea that he was saying she had so little input in the letters bearing her face and name.

"It's business, you sell your name, it's no longer yours."

"But the whole situation?"

"Well, she's more of a victim than an active agent in all of this, even if she's in the company filings, it's just the name. . . . Even if she doesn't agree with what is being done, she can't do anything about it. She would need to sue the companies to recover her own name. From the moment she sold her name, they could have been selling condoms with her name on it."

"Was this upsetting for you?"

"I'm not sure; I think for about a year and a half there have been problems. Now, they sell little medals that make you win the lotto—so for this past lotto in the USA that was a genius move. These little medals will also help you with hair loss, ingrown nails, stomach problems."

We were confused by this at first, but we realized he must have been referring to the cheap talismans sent out as part of the scam to supposedly help people win big sums of money.

"These are companies based in Switzerland. . . . They do things that are not right, with the letters you've seen, they're not right. But my mother cannot do anything about it. She can't help but go to Italy, Russia, and Japan to represent them, she's bound by a contract. In the contract, there's the actual name and there is the representation of the name, so they need a physical person, not just the name of a product; she needs to link the image and name."

This is exactly what the whistleblower had told us that Jacques was so good at—finding real people to plaster on these letters and show off to the world to make the scheme that much more believable.

"When you said there were risks, there were risks for you and your mom too? Financial?"

"Just risks."

"Have you ever spoken to these businesspeople? What do you think of them?"

"I have, yes. They are money people, who make money to make money, and more money."

"Have you spoken recently to your mother about this? Does she know we are looking into it?"

"Yes. She has her suspicions, yes."

"Suspicions? So she hasn't received our letter and phone calls?"

"Yes, but she doesn't want to respond. Like I said, she's very, very tired, very sick, and truly this has seriously affected her. It's true that after a few years she's been a little exhausted with the whole story, but she didn't have another option. She has many contracts."

"She has defended the letters in the past. Was that because of the contracts?"

"Yes, yes. Just like you are at CNN, you can't go around criticizing CNN, or you'd be sued. It's the same."

"What would happen if she tried to leave the contract?"

"She'd have to pay."

"Do you know the last time she signed a contract?"

"She's signed many contracts. It's not just one contract, there are many with many companies. Companies would have contracts with her on the name, the image, and the retention of title—I don't know how to say it in English—which is when you don't have the right to publicly or privately criticize the company. . . . She could be sued. If she wanted to buy back her name, she'd have to buy it from the company."

"And it's been twenty years since she sold it?"

"More than that—thirty years maybe. It was in the eighties. And in the beginning it was fine, the products were good."

"And why did it get bad?"

"Because of greed—because of money. When they saw the products were selling well, that the name was flourishing. . . . They started with astrology charts . . . you gave them your hour and day of birth, and it was done electronically, but she wrote the text."

"If she was in better health, do you think she'd sign another contract if she was approached?"

"I don't think she would, but does she have the choice to not sign another contract?" Again, the way he said this—his tone, his face— seemed ominous.

"If she did [have a choice]?"

"If she did, no. These companies, they are like the Godfather: 'I have an offer you cannot refuse.'"

"How quickly did she start regretting?"

"I'm not sure, but I think ten years or maybe even more. But then it was a spiral. There were things they'd ask her to do, and she couldn't say no, so it goes. You have a contract to honor, an image to care for, you have to defend the contract and the image. The great problem in this whole affair is the contract that binds her to the name, the image, and the representation."

"So you coming here to speak to us, was that a risk?"

"It depends. The things I said to you are public, but there are names, things I cannot say. . . . I don't want my mother to have any problems."

"We found in our research that this couldn't have been just one person. . . . We met people who knew your mother, and they didn't seem to describe an evil person. But all paths lead to Maria Duval."

"All paths lead to Maria Duval, the name, not the person. Between the name and the person, they're different things. Maria Duval is my mother, but physically it's her, but commercially it's not."

From everything he was telling us, we found it hard not to start feeling a tiny bit sad for Maria, a sick and elderly woman seemingly stuck in a horrible fraud. The only thing that kept us pushing back was the victims. We reminded Antoine of the millions of people, many sick and elderly just like his mother was now, who had sent their savings away in response to letters they believed were signed by her.

"It's terrible. It's terrible. But differentiate the name from the person. My mother never touched this money. There's a company and that goes to another company, and the third, and the fourth, and in the end there is no more money. There's no more."

Hearing Antoine tell it, Maria really did sound like a victim. But when Julia relayed this claim of his to us after the interview, that Maria never touched any of the money, we knew this was a flat-out lie. Unless the business filings we found were somehow mistaken, Maria had received at least several hundred thousand dollars from the scam, and she could have received far more.

And then, despite the fact that Maria had claimed in interviews that she was able to establish psychic contact through the mail, Antoine essentially acknowledged that this was not possible.

"You can't get a psychic reading from Facebook, Skype. You have to have face-to-face time, to talk to them, touch them, establish real contact. And it's not contact you can establish by mail, even though you might think about them."

While we remained skeptical of all psychic contact, even in person, it was heartening to hear that Maria Duval's son agreed it was impossible to give a true reading by mail. The crux of the US government's lawsuit rested on this fact, that the letters were a fraud because they sold this very kind of psychic contact.

"Has she ever been contacted by government authorities?"

"Yes and no. Yes because they're looking for Maria Duval, but then she tells them that Maria Duval is in fact these companies, and they go seek them."

"Physically she has spoken to them?"

"I think so, yes. Very quickly there were lawyers from the companies that would come and take over."

Our minds immediately went to our friend in Monaco. "Andrea Egger?"

"Yes, yes. And others."

"If Duval was here, what would she say to us?"

"That you have it all upside down. She's very affected by it, and she gets angry also. She's had journalists come see her, and she's said one thing and they print another. So now she doesn't want to do it anymore. She also doesn't have the right to do it."

"We think we know who started the letters—Mr. Reuille and Mr. Mailland. Is it true?"

"I think so, yes."

"And Mr. Mailland has passed away?"

"Yes, yes. And it hasn't been long. . . . When was it that we went?" Antoine turned and asked his daughter. "September, October, December? Wasn't it in June? June, yes. In Paris—but he was buried outside Paris."

"We spoke to someone who said Maria Duval is finished and Infogest is finished. Is that true?"

"The name will exist forever, and the name of the company doesn't matter."

"Patrick Guerin—do you know him?"

"Yes."

"Has Madame Duval ever met him?"

"I believe so, yes. He was well known in France, and I think he also sold his name. It's the same case."

We had considered that Patrick might be in the same boat as Maria. Jacques Mailland's Google+ profile showed Patrick as a connection. If Patrick signed some sort of contract, it made sense that Jacques could have been the one who brokered the deal.

"What did Madame Duval do with her time while she couldn't operate under her own name?"

"She couldn't do anything with her name, so she had her royalties, which is normal, but no right to use her name to do psychic readings, or work on any projects, or be on TV, if the company didn't agree with it beforehand. They asked her to do a lot of tours."

"No consultations?"

"She did it anyway because it was her passion, but only to close friends and people she had a relationship with for a while."

"So that's why we couldn't find anyone who had a consultation with her."

"No, no, but they wouldn't tell you anyway, they wouldn't say, 'Yes, I met with Madame Duval because I have a heart problem, or a work problem.'"

"Is this why she became so isolated?"

"It's been a few years now [that] she's been more distant from the world, when she moved to Callas, and it's because she's had so many terrible experiences with people. Over the past three years she's been very sick, so it's harder for her to move, and to talk, and she also has never liked to talk about her own life. It's not her thing. She liked working with people but also to do her own thing, go buy her bread unbothered. And now that's impossible. Everybody would come over to her and say, 'Maria, can you help me? Can you give me money?' There's all that."

"So were you sad to see her not able to do what she loved?"

"I was sad for her, but I knew that there was no other choice. I tried to not talk about it."

. . .

We hadn't expected our conversation at such a beautiful French café to get quite so dark.

Antoine was adamant that his mother was yet another victim of the scam—and that her name had become a runaway train that had lost its way years ago. But could that really be the case? We weren't sure what to believe.

On one hand, we knew that at the very least Maria had earned roughly $200,000 from the scam. While this was just a tiny fraction of the hundreds of millions taken in by the letters over the years, it was proof that she had received some sort of financial benefit. And for all we knew, that $200,000 could very well have been just the tip of the iceberg. That payment had been made in 2008, many years after she first started appearing on the letters. We had no way of knowing just how much she made before or after that. Antoine even admitted that he believed that his mother had been lured in with some sort of big payment to sign that first contract and that she had gone on to sign more.

Antoine remained insistent throughout the interview that his mother's main motivation was always altruistic in its intent. We suspected that her involvement could be more about her desire for fame and fortune than it was about helping people with her supposed powers. At least from all the videos and news clippings we had seen, she seemed to enjoy the attention. Antoine also claimed that Maria didn't know how to use a computer, making it plausible that Maria didn't realize how big the scam had grown.

Either way, if Antoine's story was even partially true, it explained a lot.

It explained why employees of the companies sending out the letters claimed to have seen only glimpses of Maria. Why the letters were sent in languages she didn't speak. Why she became so elusive and isolated. And why she was afraid to talk to us.

Before our meeting with Antoine, we had answered the main question we'd originally set out to find. From the town hall sighting of her with the pot of jelly and the man who claimed to have installed her pool to our conversations with her sister and her son, we were now confident Maria was a living, breathing person. It was her name that had become a multimillion-dollar work of fiction.

The three of us walked in silence through the dark alleys of Toulon as we made our way back to our car. At one point, we noticed a group of young men who seemed to be following us and for a moment, we worried we were about to be mugged and would lose all our notes from the trip and the precious audio recording of the conversation with Antoine. But Julia was undeterred, yelling curse words at them in French, which seemed to do the trick.

On the drive home, Julia played the recording of our interview with Antoine from the back seat of the car, stopping it every few seconds to give us direct translations. We had apparently missed some interesting details during the actual meeting, as Julia had become so enthralled by the conversation that her English translations were less and less frequent. She told us something that thoroughly intrigued us that we hadn't caught before: Maria had been close enough to Jacques to be invited to his funeral, and, as we learned, so was her family. This made us even more curious about the nature of Maria and Jacques's relationship. Was Antoine more involved with the businessmen than he'd made it seem?

Our time in Callas tracking down the mysterious Maria Duval had come to an end. As we boarded our flight back home we couldn't stop agonizing over the competing theories we had formed about Maria Duval.

Had the woman at the center of this scam really become its most unexpected victim, as Antoine had told us? Or had she been an eager participant in the scheme all along, preying off other people's grief, fueled by her own greed and ego?

At the time, we were convinced it could be only one or the other, forgetting that in life there are often shades of gray.

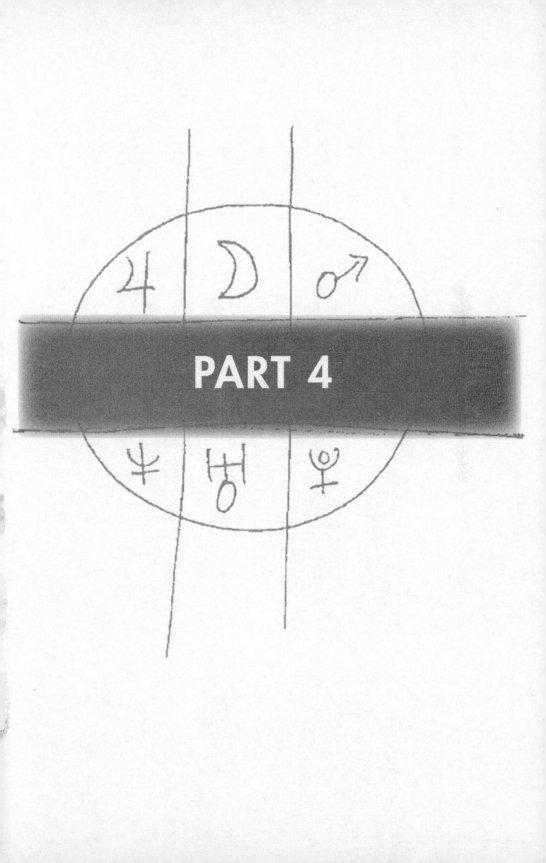

PART 4

The Myth

MARIA'S LETTERS ALWAYS made a huge deal about her supposed ability to find missing people. In France we were stunned when the archivist from the local newspaper pulled out the decades-old article claiming she'd found an elderly man using only a photo that his family provided.

We were dubious about the claim, though the clipping at least showed that she really did make headlines as someone who could locate the missing. We still hadn't seen any evidence of the one story that kept popping up: the unbelievable rescue of the missing person in the ritzy resort town of Saint-Tropez. Her website had detailed the story, as told by a so-called skeptic, who had also been mesmerized by her catlike eyes. This person had described Maria and this discovery in great detail, but we were never able to track down his or her identity. In a YouTube video Maria told a similar story, which Antoine had seemed to mention again in the Toulon café. But there was one big discrepancy between their versions and the one from her website. Maria and Antoine talked about her finding a man, while the website recounted the rescue of a missing dentist's wife.

We had shown the friendly archivist at *Nice-Matin* a newspaper headline that a fan had posted online. When he couldn't find the paper that should've shown the headline, we became convinced the story was a myth, as we'd initially assumed. If it were a photoshopped image used to lure in more victims, that would explain why the subject of the alleged rescue had morphed depending on who was telling the story.

Once we were back in the States, the friendly archivist told us he'd found another article. It wasn't the one we'd been looking for in the archives. This one, from 1978, was all about Maria's various rescues over the years, glorifying her as "the nicest of the witches."

Local police and firefighters don't hesitate to give Maria Duval a call after their regular efforts fail. She is always available and her pendulum is almost always right.

It was clear that whoever wrote the article thought highly of Maria, saying that she greeted the author from a street by her garden, which was soaked in sunlight and filled with zodiac signs.

It could be that one day we will witness the birth of the Witch Liberation Movement, and if they choose a flag-bearer, it will certainly be the nicest and most lovely of them all, Maria Duval of Draguignan—next to her, the old-timey images of witches with brooms, crooked fingers and noses are ridiculous.

Then we noticed a mention of Saint-Tropez.

Two years ago in Saint-Tropez, the wife of a doctor went missing, and all the search parties had been fruitless. The population, the vacationers, were in upheaval when a young woman came to the police.

The woman was Maria, who according to the article asked for a photo of the woman and a map of the country, which authorities set up on a table in front of her.

> *They all saw, at the end of a few minutes, the pendulum, until then moving, coming to a stop and stabilizing over a precise point.*
> *"She's here," said the young lady.*
> *Just in case, a helicopter [was sent] to the place indicated, not far from Gassin. The woman was there, hurt and unable to move.*

There it was, practically word for word, the same story we'd kept hearing—but again, with one key difference. This article mentioned a doctor's wife instead of a dentist's wife, like the story from Maria's website. We had always assumed that the tale on her website was written by some creative copywriter. But perhaps it was actually a sloppy translation of one of these newspaper articles. The difference in the two stories really did all come down to one French word. This still didn't explain, though, why Maria and Antoine had told the exact same story about a missing man rather than a woman. We still had a lot of questions and had a hard time believing that Maria could have found anyone with simply a pendulum.

The article also included a number of other personal details about the psychic that we had seen in her letters but had ruled out as fiction. It talked about her ability to find missing animals, reminding us of how her letters claimed she had found Brigitte Bardot's dog and of a trademark we once found for what appeared to be a business producing horoscopes for dogs. It said she had spent her childhood in Italy, raised by a family who had their own psychic powers. This included her uncle, a priest in a small village near Milan "who told her once, before she could understand it, that the golden strands inside her brown eyes gave her the power of communication." It also said she had been examined by authorities who determined she truly was a psychic. Again, this all matched the letters, while the story of her uncle also mirrored what Maria had supposedly written in the book that Françoise sent us (though in the book her eyes had been described as green). The numerous small details in the article also matched much of what Antoine had told us, such as the fact that Maria had worked in art galleries and that she'd gone through several divorces.

This article had a familiar byline. It was the name of a man who had written other positive articles about Maria. His writing seemed suspiciously similar to that of the self-proclaimed skeptic on her website. But as we searched online and enlisted the newspaper's help to try to locate him, we couldn't find any evidence of his current existence or a way to contact him. The people mentioned in his various articles were also nowhere to be found in our online searches. Without talking to this writer, it was impossible for us to verify that anything he had written was actually true, as the supposed rescues had happened decades ago. But his articles, published in a widely read reputable newspaper, seemed to have helped make Maria famous. They had convinced people for years that she was the real deal, everyone from locals in town to the newspaper archivist to the millions of victims who read these stories over and over again.

Early in our journey, we had been convinced that Maria Duval was nothing more than a stock image. Once we determined she existed, we believed the letters were pure fabrications and we still doubted her powers. Real or not, however, the myth of Maria Duval was rooted in more than a copywriter's wild imagination.

The Responses

Maria Duval is a living, breathing woman. And she really was known around France for her psychic gifts.

It's her name that has become a multimillion-dollar work of fiction. And it is this name that could live on forever—or for as long as people are getting rich from it.

This is how our series on CNN ended, when it was published over a six-week period in the winter of 2016, while the US presidential debates and primary season were in full swing. But this wasn't where the Maria Duval story stopped.

Our obsession had spanned nearly half a year, and we were relieved to get the story of Maria Duval out into the world so we could move on with our lives. Shortly after our series ran, the US government announced it had finally shut down the massive Maria Duval scheme for good, after more than a decade of effort. A settlement was reached that Maria herself allegedly signed.

We quickly began an entirely different investigation, this one into a modeling agency run by Donald Trump, then a presidential candidate. Our investigation found that Trump's agency had profited from the very same visa program for foreign workers that he slammed in his campaign, and immigration attorneys told us that the agency appeared to have violated federal law. From there, we looked into the modeling industry as a whole, finding that labor abuses ran rampant throughout the industry. As we pored through visa records and interviewed countless financially exploited models, though, our email inboxes were being hijacked by people from all around the world who wanted to talk about one thing: Maria Duval.

At first, the bulk of these messages came from victims and family members who wanted to share their own stories of drained bank accounts and outrage. Others came from armchair detectives whose curiosity had prompted them to do their own research and develop entirely new theories about Maria and the scam, some of which they posted online. A woman claiming to be a signature analyst, for example, posted a nearly nine-minute-long YouTube video about Maria's signature, saying that the "M" suggested that Maria was a "devious" individual—going so far as to compare her signature to Hitler's. Still more messages came from people with intriguing inside knowledge, which took us beyond Maria and into the world of mail fraud. There we found scammer after scammer who had created the kinds of letters that had filled Doreen's mailbox for years, reminiscent of the same letters that started us on this journey in the first place.

The Other Psychics

AMID THE FLOOD of emails that were landing in our special-investigations inbox every day was a brief message from a French "astropsychologist" who called himself Dr. Turi.

"Do not throw the baby with the water!"

We initially overlooked this message, confused about what this person was trying to tell us. But then we noticed a blog post Dr. Turi had written. The rambling missive began with an apocalyptic GIF of fiery clouds and a quote warning his readers that the universe is "under no obligation to make any SPIRITUAL sense to anyone."

In the post, he blasted our story as an attack on the entire spiritual and psychic world, calling us innocent "kids" who knew little of "the mysterious world they live in." Then he went on to tell a personal story about his own experience with psychic mailings, in which he described an arrangement similar to the one Antoine had told us about Maria. We were hesitant to enter into a battle of words with this man, but our curiosity got the best of us. So we sent him an email asking if he would speak with us.

Thank you for taking some of your precious time to answer my email. Be sure my world wide reading audience will enjoy this "debate" fully were [*sic*] I will offer solid proofs of my cosmic gift!

We immediately began to regret our decision when we were subsequently bombarded with emails from his followers telling us about aliens, government cover-ups, the alignment of the moon and the stars, and how Dr. Turi had used his gift to change their lives. Apparently he had spread our email address far and wide, urging his supporters to get in touch. We called him anyway.

When he didn't answer his phone, we left a voice mail. Then we received an email from his wife, Mrs. Turi, who seemed skeptical of our motives and protective of her husband. Eventually we were able to get on the phone with both of them, and the phone call was one of the weirdest we had ever experienced. Dr. Turi and his wife often spoke over each other, at some points bickering dramatically. He patronizingly shushed her on multiple occasions, talked in circles, and was difficult to follow.

He told us he had became trapped in a terrible business deal after signing a contract with a Canadian marketing company just a few years earlier. He said the company had called and asked him if he wanted to sign a contract that would allow it to use his "name and worldwide reputation" to promote its business. The company flew him and his wife to Toronto, put them up in a fancy hotel, wined and dined them, showed them around the office and shipment facility, and gave them a tour of the city. The trip ended with a meeting in the president's office, where Dr. Turi signed a contract.

He also explained much of this in multiple posts on his website, writing, for instance:

I was certain my astrological expertise would serve a real solid purpose and as always, my unarguable, well-documented, dated predictions would be recognized as legitimate.

After a few weeks, I received the sample to what was going to be mailed to hundreds of thousands people all over the world from Canada! To our dismay, NOTHING of what I sent them was used! Instead my solid daily guidance and predictions forecasts were turned into the very same type of deceptive Neptunian gibberish found in the CNN article [a reference to the Maria Duval letters he'd learned about from our article]. [The letters] used my name and my picture into a very famous psychic promising to find love, to win the lottery, to find lost pets and a myriad of nonsense that infuriated me for months to come.

This all sounded very similar to what we had heard about Maria. Dr. Turi thought he would be able to offer some sort of valid service via the mail since he'd willingly signed a contract. Just like Maria, he claimed not to have realized what he was getting himself into.

On top of this, he told us that he received only a few hundred dollars in royalties. He told us he got out of the contract as soon as he could, but the damage was done: many of the ardent followers he'd attracted over his years of work thought he was a scammer.

"I've been conned," he told us.

• • •

We still didn't know what to think of Dr. Turi, but we began to see how someone could end up at the center of a scam beyond his or her control. His story also gave us a window into the booming business of mail-order psychics, indicating once again that sometimes all it takes for a shady company to profit is a compelling face and name. It made us think of Patrick, the psychic whose letter we'd found all those months ago in the pile of junk mail. It seemed that, like Maria and Dr. Turi, he too was also a living person.

During our research into the businessmen involved with Maria, we'd come across a number of other psychics with their own supposed talents, personalities, and backstories. They all followed a strikingly similar pattern, and some of their websites and letters were almost identical. There was the elderly clairvoyant named Laetizia, who claimed to come from a long line of psychics on her family's small Mediterranean island. A young woman wearing a brightly colored sari named Alisha boasted that she'd helped thousands of people solve their problems. And a blue-eyed girl named Rinalda said she'd received her psychic gift after falling into a coma from a terrible bout of appendicitis.

All three of these supposed psychics had websites that claimed they could help people win money or find love, just as the letters from Maria and Patrick did, and as those from Dr. Turi apparently did as well. The websites also happened to trace back to our Swiss friend with the Sparks mailboxes, Martin Dettling. While we could find the stray complaint online about these three female psychics, for the most part they seemed to have gained little traction compared with the massive success and notoriety of the Maria Duval letters.

We also discovered a young, handsome Swiss man who lived a secret life in Panama. With long, highlighted hair and earrings, Martin Zoller claimed on his website that he'd risen to international fame after using his psychic skills to find a missing plane in the jungles of Bolivia. Martin's website was flashy and highly produced, and it appeared he had followers on social media who attended various events he hosted. He offered psychic guidance for a fee—but unlike Maria, his messages were sent by email, and he had never been publicly accused of any sort of wrongdoing. And again, one of the companies behind his psychic empire had its own Maria Duval connections. It was managed by a Swiss businessman tied to the scheme, and we soon found evidence that its main shareholder had made a donation to a nonprofit as a wedding gift for Jean-Claude Reuille, our pen pal living in Thailand.

The most interesting of the psychic bunch was a woman named Anne Chamfort—another supposedly "world-famous" French clairvoyant. We first heard her name from our Astroforce whistleblower source, who said that she had been one of three psychic personas used by Jacques Mailland in the early years. Her name also appeared alongside Maria's in online complaints from many years ago, but it seemed that her name had gone dormant as Maria became the star.

When our stories about the Maria letters hit the internet, an anonymous source contacted us with some interesting information. She said she worked for a direct marketing company headquartered in Moscow that was currently sending out letters and psychic readings signed by Anne Chamfort. The source said it was clear that the Anne Chamfort letters were modeled directly after Maria's and that they were currently being sent out in the Philippines, Vietnam, Indonesia, South Africa, and Russia. "Anne Chamfort's letters are just copy-paste versions of Duval's letters," she told us. "Take out Duval's photos and stick in Chamfort's."

Interestingly, the Russian company listed on domain registrations for AnneChamfort.com was the same company that owned Maria's Russian website domain. And just like Maria, a woman claiming to be Anne Chamfort traveled the world with her psychic predictions. Just as our articles were publishing, several media reports heralded her arrival in Vietnam—though we found little evidence that she gained international traction after that.

All these psychics were just some of the ones we found who had clear connections to Maria Duval and the businesspeople involved in her scheme—though they hadn't faced government actions like her letters had or to our knowledge ever been charged with wrongdoing. From all the family members of victims we spoke with, we learned that there were dozens of other mail-order psychics bombarding the elderly with promises of big winnings and good luck.

For some reason, none of these psychics had become nearly as powerful—or valuable—as Maria.

The Checks

WEEKS AFTER PUBLISHING our investigation, we set our sights on a little-known Canadian company cashing checks for the Maria Duval scam.

PacNet Services, we learned, had profited from all kinds of global mail fraud for years. As we embarked on another months-long investigation, this time into PacNet, we discovered that we weren't the only ones interested in it. In fact, on the same day that our story was eventually published, the US government took an unprecedented action against this very company, labeling it a "significant transnational criminal organization" and landing it on the same short list as some of the world's most notorious gangs and drug cartels.

This designation may sound extreme, but after years of trying to shut down individual scams one at a time, the government's effort had become a game of Whack-a-Mole. As soon as one was shut down, another would pop up in its place. Government officials hoped that by shutting down PacNet, they would shut down the scams as well.

To truly understand how an obscure payment processor ended up on a list of criminals, you first have to understand how PacNet worked.

Operating out of a nondescript high-rise in downtown Vancouver, British Columbia, PacNet made it possible for con artists to shield their operations from authorities and get their hands on millions of dollars sent in from victims using bank accounts set up in PacNet's own name. In the case of someone like Doreen, the process would start when she received a letter, maybe one telling her she'd won $1 million. All she needed to do, the letter insisted, was to send in $20 to claim this life-changing prize. The letter looked official, so she would get out her checkbook and mail that $20.

Payments like these often ended up with PacNet, which then deposited the money into an account under its own name and took a cut as a commission. It then held on to the rest of the funds, until they were eventually sent to the client's own bank account. There were so many layers to this crime that victims typically had no idea that PacNet was even involved, except in rare cases where frustrated family members found fine print on the back of canceled checks and traced the deposits to PacNet.

Throughout our investigation, PacNet repeatedly claimed to us that it never knowingly facilitated fraud, despite the fact we found scam after scam that was processed by the company. But the US government ultimately found that PacNet was part of a massive global network of shady businesses and con artists that made their fortunes from mail fraud. Many of the schemes were remarkably similar, raking in millions each year by sending out letters that tricked people into thinking they'd won the lottery or found a psychic adviser like Maria.

Over time, we began to notice familiar faces and suspicious connections among the scammers and the businesses that helped them. We called these individuals "the mail fraud mafia." In this world, people connected to the Maria Duval letters just kept popping up.

Every year, many of them rendezvoused at an annual gathering in some of the world's most exclusive resort towns. The conferences, sponsored by PacNet, were held in such settings as a five-star floating "yacht hotel" in Gibraltar; around the mountains of Whistler, British Columbia; and the beachfront of Marbella, Spain, and they featured activities like Sangria-making competitions, Flamenco performances, and extravagant dinners lasting into the early morning. We let our imaginations run wild thinking of what these gatherings must have been like, picturing fraudsters trading sucker lists full of victims like candy and toasting future million-dollar scams over flutes of expensive champagne.

Old attendance lists from the conference contained key executives of the Canadian Infogest (the company that had been in charge of the Maria Duval operations in North America), the curly-haired copywriter who'd written some of her letters, and a number of other names from the sprawling business web we'd pieced together months earlier. It was in the records of this conference that Jacques Mailland's name showed up as an attendee of the Marbella gathering.

Once again, there was a connection everywhere we looked.

The Dark and the Strange

THE MARIA DUVAL story had led us to the colorful astropsychologist Dr. Turi, with his own story of how he had been conned, to all the Maria Duval copycats out there hawking their own psychic services, to the company cashing the checks, and to the mail fraud mafia. And now it was leading us in a direction that seemed a whole lot darker.

It all started with an email that left us particularly unsettled. Throughout the following months, the cryptic messages and inquiries would continue, making us feel less and less like journalists on the outside looking in. Instead, we were becoming a central part of the story ourselves.

I have information that will shed a lot more light onto this mystery, though, I regret to say, the truth is far more frightening than you might have imagined. Please confirm that I've reached the correct person and that this is your best email. Then I will elaborate further. Thank you.

That was the first email we received. It came out of nowhere and we couldn't figure out if it had any connection to our investigation, but it added to the growing sense of darkness surrounding this scam.

Intrigued and slightly terrified, we quickly responded to the sender, letting him know he had reached the right people. In the days that followed, we exchanged emails and talked at length on the phone. The sender, who claimed to be a documentary filmmaker, told us an outlandish theory that was unlike anything else we had heard.

When he read our stories, he said they had immediately reminded him of something he'd learned years ago while working on a documentary on the history of cults. While conducting interviews for the film, he was introduced to a European therapist who allegedly helped cult victims recover from trauma. The therapist was in his eighties when they met. He told the filmmaker about the times when he'd gone undercover to study the inner workings of cults and religious organizations. He mentioned something else that the filmmaker says was shocking and impossible to forget.

According to the fantastical and unsubstantiated story he had heard, the Maria Duval scam was linked to a highly secretive organization dedicated to the dark arts dating back to the 1800s and concentrated mainly in Europe. He didn't know how to spell or pronounce the name, but said he believed it was something like "Krinig." Its main mission? "They intently want to create negative acts, reverse karma. They believe that if you do bad things, good things will happen," he said. Given the group's interest in astrology and black magic, psychics like Maria had unknowingly become ensnared in its web—the perfect vehicles to help the organization prey on the weak and make money in the process.

According to this theory:

When the organization came into Duval's life, they further reinforced and enabled her delusional belief of being a psychic. At that point, getting her to partake in [the] scam was easy—because she didn't see it as a scam. Brainwashing an average person into believing and doing certain things is far less efficient than reinforcing an existing delusional self-image. Why bother creating a Maria Duval from scratch when they could empower and enable an existing one?

Based on what he had been told, the filmmaker doubted that Maria had any idea what she was getting herself into, and he suspected that only the organization's highest members understood the full picture and magnitude of what was at play.

Each person has a specific task to make it work. Each person gets a certain amount of limited information. None of them see the big picture. They never have enough information to bring it down. It was all very strange. . . . To this day I have no idea what happened to him. I finally decided to put all of it behind me and went on with my life.

It almost sounded like the Illuminati, the mythical society we'd stumbled across after looking into the other secretive organizations Maria's son, Antoine, was involved with.

At the time the filmmaker was told this story, he couldn't believe what he was hearing, and he asked the therapist why he hadn't gone to the authorities.

He said doing so was both useless and dangerous. There was no hard target for the authorities to zero [in] on, and any attempt to expose the people behind it would endanger his daughter and grandchildren. He didn't allow me to make copies of what he showed me, record it, or even take notes.

We couldn't wait to have our own conversation with this therapist, already compiling a list of questions as the wild tale unfolded. We asked the filmmaker how we could get in touch with this man.

He told us that the therapist had disappeared from his life just as mysteriously as he had entered it.

About three months after my last conversation I called again and his phone was disconnected. When I called the woman who had introduced us, a family member told me that she had died in a car accident. It was all very strange. . . . To this day I have no idea what happened to him. I finally decided to put all of it behind me and went on with my life.

Then, years later, he read our stories. Suddenly all these memories came rushing back, leading him to create his own theories about Maria and the scam. While he could offer absolutely no proof of these claims, his theory had become quite detailed.

There's nothing surprising about Duval being reclusive. She knows about her handlers and revealing anything would put her family in danger. I think that at some point something occurred that made her "snap out of it" and realize the gravity of what she was part of, but by then it was too late. This is just my opinion. It's important to think about why an organization would perpetrate such a cruel, sinister scam. Money is merely the end result.

This sounded a lot like Antoine's reference to *The Godfather* when he described why his mother was so afraid to get out of her contracts. Now it seemed more than just a dramatic metaphor.

The concept of this scam is simple, but making it work without leaving actionable evidence is a complex process that would have to require the cooperation of many people on many levels, and such cooperation requires a mutual belief system. The repercussions of this scam [for] its victims would have to be as important to this organization as the money, otherwise it would never work. If there are copycat scams, they're managed by the same organization in order to confuse and dilute any one potential target, and based on what [the therapist] told me, it's hardly their only illicit business venture.

He insisted that we dig deeper. "You found the music, but not the orchestra."

Our conversations with the filmmaker were the most alarming yet. Somehow, our investigation into a case of consumer fraud had led us to theories of a satanic cult hiding in the shadows for centuries.

When we hung up and debriefed, we considered if this could somehow be the missing piece of the puzzle that had eluded us all along. Perhaps it could explain how the scam had managed to last so long, the true motivations of the international fraud, and why Maria felt so trapped—and why she was terrified to tell us what had really happened. After all, the filmmaker had told us that if anyone tried to get out of the tight-knit cult or alert anyone to its inner workings, the consequences would be extreme.

The cult story was such a far-flung theory that we couldn't rely on a secondhand account from a man we didn't even know, about a conversation from years ago. There was always the chance that the therapist had some reason for making up this whole story. Or maybe the filmmaker was simply out of his mind or had his own motivations for duping us. It wouldn't have been the first time a reporter was purposely taken for ride, and we would need some substantial proof before we would ever label any of this as fact. Still, we weren't ready to dismiss the idea without making our own attempts to find evidence. And it was definitely one of the more interesting and disturbing detours on this already unconventional journey. Even as we were still on the phone with the filmmaker, we quickly began searching for any trace of the word "Krinig." We tried every spelling we could think of, but we found nothing.

In the weeks that followed our April conversation with the filmmaker, we continued to look for Krinig, reaching out to cult experts around the world. One of these experts, a German journalist who had spent decades digging into obscure religions and exposing ritual abuse, polled more than one hundred people in her field, but no one had heard the name.

We then searched for any information about the therapist, hoping that the filmmaker was wrong and that this man was out there somewhere for us to speak with ourselves. The filmmaker recalled that the therapist was from Europe and was apparently living in California when the two of them met. We proceeded to search public records for his name and looked online for any evidence of his supposed decades of work. In our experience as reporters, we knew that if someone lived in the United States, even for a relatively short period of time, he or she could be traced.

We found no evidence this man ever existed.

The journalist and cult expert we'd corresponded with was from Germany, where the therapist had allegedly studied and worked, so we asked her if she had heard of him. On a Skype call with her one morning, we explained that the elderly therapist had supposedly been born in Croatia but had spent most of his career in Berlin and New York. We told her how the filmmaker even claimed he'd brought two official-looking diplomas to their meeting, including one from a German university.

The German journalist said that she had worked in this very niche field, also helping cult survivors, for many years. She had never heard his name. She also found the details of his biography very suspicious. "This is a bit weird, a Croatian man coming to Germany to study after the war," she said. "Sounds like a bit of a crazy story. It can happen, but doesn't sound very likely." She also told us that as far as she knew, the university where he supposedly studied didn't have a medical school, but that perhaps it could have in the past. Or it was possible that he had come to Germany with a medical degree from Croatia.

After we hung up, she did some more digging of her own, even contacting the German university. In a detailed email, she told us she confirmed that there was never a medical school there, only a psychology institute, which focused on business psychology studies. "In principle it would have been possible to study psychology, but shortly after the war they focused on business affairs, not healing and supporting trauma victims," she wrote.

"As far as I know it was not uncommon that people from Europe, who moved to the States, did some 'colouring' or 'shape-lift' with their CVs to find a job and start a new life," she said in her email. "So maybe he studied psychology for business and started 'learning by doing' to work with survivors. Maybe he even made a doctor's degree on the base of a business psychology education, who knows. As long as he did good work."

That was the problem—despite all our efforts, we still couldn't verify that he had done any of the work he'd allegedly told the filmmaker about. Or that he was even a real person.

The therapist was a ghost.

Unable to find any proof of this supposed cult's existence or that any of the businessmen were remotely involved in a satanic group, we looked back to everything we had gathered about Maria to see if there were any clues we'd missed. Buried in the same article that detailed her alleged Saint-Tropez rescue of the doctor's wife was a paragraph we'd skimmed over before.

We now found it chilling.

She's at the center of a friend circle of 13 people just as passionate about strange and mysterious things, who all possess indubitable gifts. "We evolve spiritually by using all that we were given by 'the forces' to obtain all sorts of things."

The paragraph in the article describing Maria's involvement in a circle of friends "passionate about strange and mysterious things" seemed like a questionable coincidence. The article alone was hardly enough to conclude that Maria was part of a cult or that the organization existed at all. It did, however, give us insight into how she could have justified the letters to herself.

This quote from her seemed especially telling:

"Material possessions are not in contradiction with spirituality."

· · ·

More creepy messages and warnings continued to land in our in-boxes. One came from someone who called himself a "Secret Friend" and emailed from an address that seemed to have been created exclusively to communicate with us. This anonymous tipster told us about a man he believed was the leader of the scam's business operations in North America.

"[He is] a little crazy and unpredictable and I'd rather stay safe," the secret friend wrote. "Dig deeper, Blake. Good luck.—A friend"

Another message came from someone who claimed to have worked for the Maria Duval operations in the early years. He told us about a man who'd worked closely with Jacques Mailland and was in charge of sending out a number of psychic mailings. He even claimed that this man's wife was the original face of the Anne Chamfort scam, whose letters we noticed were beginning to resurface. This source didn't mention anything that was particularly alarming. But when we searched the man's name online, one of the first comments about him raised our eyebrows.

"[He] is a dangerous man, ready to pay for detective and will prosecute you if you are too near his business. He drives a Ferrari and a Rolls-Royce," someone had written many years ago on Astrocat, a trusty forum we had used for months now.

We'd long thought of the men behind the scheme as nothing more than white-collar criminals. It was from our meeting with Antoine that we began to suspect that they might be far more nefarious. But with these email warnings, now more than ever, we were concerned about our safety, and cautious about the path we were going down.

. . .

Another strange missive opened our eyes to an entirely different side of Maria.

Throughout our investigation, we had come across a number of references suggesting that Maria had a connection to Argentina, thousands of miles away from her home in France. Early in our reporting, as we reached out to government agencies around the world,

Australian officials had told us a Singaporean man named Tony had been claiming that Maria spent time in Argentina. Later, Julia had uncovered official government documents suggesting Maria owned some sort of property there.

We had pictured this property as just another one of her glamorous villas and had never spent too much time trying to get to the bottom of it. But we began to reconsider things after hearing from a man claiming that Maria's connection to Argentina was in fact an empty field. It started with an email in which he said that he had been scammed by Maria.

> Dear Sirs CNN:
>
> My name is Luis Alberto Ramos I am from Argentina. I have thoroughly read your truthful investigation about Mme Duval.
>
> If it were of your interest, I could send you checkable accurate and precise information about the scam I was victim of, and of the consequent legal public processes I had to face against Maria Duval (a flesh and bones person).
>
> At your disposal.
>
> Yours,
>
> Mr. LUIS ALBERTO RAMOS

By now, we were used to hearing from victims of Maria, but this time, the story had nothing to do with her psychic powers or letters.

This man, whom we came to call Mr. Ramos, told us he was currently embroiled in a years-long legal battle against Maria, claiming that she had defrauded him. He said he sold Maria a field in Argentina but that she'd never paid him for the property or the machinery on it. Utterly confused and convinced we were misunderstanding him, we asked what kind of field Maria had purchased from him.

Mr. Ramos said it was farmland used for raising cattle that came with cows, machinery, and a waterfall, but that Maria used it to con him. Maria's son, Antoine, disputed this whole story, however, saying that it was the other way around. He said Mr. Ramos actually owed Maria money. Mr. Ramos and his attorney later elaborated on what went wrong with the deal, saying that Maria had bought the property in the late nineties with a significant other and stopped making payments when they split up. They said the payments had been peculiar from the beginning, coming from bank accounts in a number of different countries including Canada, the United States, and France.

Mr. Ramos still doesn't understand why Maria bought the land from him in the first place. She didn't live in a house on the land she purchased or have any family there. He said the lawsuit continued to stretch on, but that he had not seen her in person since 1999.

"I met her SEVERAL times in flesh, bone, and blood. She is a real human being," he wrote. She was "a quite good-looking, charming woman. Blond (or dyed), blue nice eyes, pretty lips, 60" [around five feet]." He also wrote that she acted mysteriously about her powers, likening her to a "scaramouche," a character in commedia dell'arte who is seen as a boastful coward who gets himself in tricky situations but somehow manages to escape.

The Romanians

M ONTHS PASSED AND we heard nothing.

It was August, and most of the days' headlines focused on Donald Trump, who had secured the Republican nomination for president. We were deep in our newest investigation into PacNet, which needed our full attention after the firm hired a prominent US lawyer to threaten to sue us.

But when an email popped up from someone in Romania, we couldn't help but be intrigued.

From: ████████████████████
Sent: Sunday, August 7, 2016 6:31 AM
To: Ellis, Blake
Subject: Maria Dunal [*sic*] in Romania

Hallo!

My name is ████████████████████. I'm a reporter in Romania.

Maria Duval is here. Yes, it [*sic*] here. She works for a company. I have evidence of this. But . . .

I need your help. I need copies of the documents collected: photo-

graphs, letters, testimonials customers Maria Duval etc. for a special
TV report.

For all this will give the address Maria Duval in Romania, including
photos of the new look of Maria Duval. She looks different now. But the
voice and face are unmistakable.

The new name: Madame Duval.

Type scam: letters and advertisements (talismans, books, amulets,
crystals, etc.)

Our first instinct was to help this reporter. We too had been helped
by international journalists who had done their own research on Maria's letters. Cautious about turning over our notebooks to a stranger,
though, we first sent him a copy of the public US lawsuit, which had
plenty of letters and other information. In return, he sent us a twenty-
seven-page PDF full of photos of Maria, her talismans, and copies of
letters we hadn't seen before. One image was especially curious, since
it seemed to be a photo of Maria that had run online as part of our
story but that someone had doctored in order to make her appear to be
holding a crystal ball. The picture made us wonder: Could scammers
be using the details from our story to try to copycat the scheme in
other countries?

We quickly responded and asked where the reporter had gotten
all of this information, and whether he could still share the address
he said he had for Maria in Romania.

Then he disappeared.

We searched his name online and couldn't find anything, which
was especially odd since he claimed to be a journalist. We emailed
him again asking where he worked and when his piece would be published, but still no response.

Then, another email came in from Romania just two days later.

But this one wasn't from the reporter. Attached to the message was a photo we'd included in our story—a copy of the note we had written by hand and left for Maria in her mailbox while in France seven months earlier. Strangely, this email seemed to have been written directly in response to our note.

> From: ███████████████████
> Sent: Tuesday, August 09, 2016 11:31 AM
> To: Ellis, Blake
> Subject: For Blake Ellis
>
> Reply to your message (image attached).
>   For questions about Maria Duval please contact me.
>   ██████████████████: Secretary "Office Express" ® 2016 in Romania—Maria Duval

What? Our story had been up for months. Why were we suddenly getting multiple emails from Romania? And why would Maria have a secretary in Romania? We thought that maybe this woman and the reporter were somehow working together or were potentially the same person. We seriously questioned their motivations. If they were copycat scammers, were they trying to get more material from us to use in their letters? Or was this some sort of prank? We had our doubts, but we responded anyway, asking the woman if she worked directly for Maria or whether she was tasked with sending out letters on her behalf. We also asked what "Office Express" was and whether she would be willing to speak with us over the phone.

> From: ██████████████████████████
> Date: August 11, 2016 at 9:56:39 AM MDT

To: "Ellis, Blake"
Subject: Re: For Blake Ellis

Warning!
    The requested information is confidential (I signed a contract with
Maria Duval and Office® Express-Romania).
    Thank you !

We wrote back multiple times, but just as with the Romanian
journalist, we never heard from her again.

The Childhood Friend

W E WERE KNEE deep into a new investigation—this time an even more unrelated project exposing rampant sexual abuse in nursing homes—when we received another message, from a man named Patric, that had us wondering if someone was up to his old tricks.

> Hello
>> You want now [*sic*] if Maria Duval exist?
>> Yes
>> I now [*sic*] her

Unlike the people who'd emailed us from Romania, Patric was happy to get on the phone, sending us his number right away. When we spoke with him, he told us he was a childhood friend of Jean-Claude Reuille's, that he had known him for forty years, and that he'd met Maria Duval multiple times. After telling us this in English, he said he would prefer to speak in French, so we enlisted the help of our colleague Julia, who was still as interested in this whole saga as we were, and who quickly spoke with Patric on the phone.

We were in disbelief as we read through the rough notes of her conversation.

PATRIC: *So you want to know if she exists? She does. I can confirm she exists.*

JULIA: *Do you know her in person?*

PATRIC: *Yes, I know her very well.*

JULIA: *Oh, really?*

PATRIC: *Yes, but all I can say is that she is real. I can say she's real. She's fantastic, in fact. Incredible.*

JULIA: *And how do you know her?*

PATRIC: *Through Jean-Claude.*

JULIA: *Because they worked together?*

PATRIC: *Well, that's what you want to know, isn't it?*

JULIA: *Yes.*

PATRIC: (Laughs) *I don't know . . .*

JULIA: *Yes, of course you know . . . We know a lot about her already. Maybe not the same things you know. But we know she exists, that she lives in the South of France, that—*

PATRIC: *Yes, I saw that you went to her house.*

JULIA: *Yes, and we are currently in talks with her son, so we know she exists, that she is a psychic, and a great astrologist, but we want to know how she became famous, what happened to get her from a small-town radio guest and having a column in the newspaper to the person she became, giving talks around the world.*

PATRIC: *You know how that happened. It was with Jean-Claude.*

The conversation went on for a while, during which time Patric offered Julia a number of other interesting tidbits. He said that Maria "wouldn't have been in business without Jean-Claude" but that she too had made a lot of money, which she'd mismanaged and spent on "stupid things and young men." He even explained the backstory of property records we'd found in Argentina, saying that Maria had fallen in love with a young man who'd convinced her to buy property there, making us wonder if he was referring to the field in Argentina that Maria had allegedly purchased from Mr. Ramos.

With even more stories to tell, he suggested we meet in person.

"I know his life very well. Listen, JC has had many business operations with Maria Duval, all over the world, so it's a personal thing too."

This all seemed very suspicious. While some of what he said matched what we already knew, and he used the nickname "JC" that Jean-Claude himself had used to sign many of the emails he sent us, we questioned why Patric was getting in touch now and what he had to gain from it.

The same day, Julia heard from him again. "Patric just called me," she emailed us. "He hadn't spoken to Reuille in 3 years, but says now that Reuille wants to meet . . . in February or March location tbd." When we asked for more information, Julia sent the following message:

> So for meeting Reuille, Patric said it would likely not be in the US—
> *IF* he can leave Thailand (which Patric says he might not be able to because of legal trouble), he would likely want to meet up somewhere in Europe.

Again, we were confused. We had been in touch with Jean-Claude directly by email. He could just have let us know himself that he wanted to meet in person. And Patric was clearly suggesting that Jean-Claude was much more involved than he'd previously admitted. We needed to reach Jean-Claude ourselves to ask him about Patric.

That's when things got even stranger.

Jean-Claude seemed confused by our message, asking us to tell him more about his "friend" Patric, claiming he didn't know anyone by that name.

"I do not know any Patric, but I know one Patrice and two Patric*k*. The 3 of them were involved in Mail Order business. However I did not talk to any of them for at least 2 years," he wrote. "Anyway, if I want to meet you, I do not see why I would need anyone to help me. I would just call you or email you. But, I have absolutely nothing to add [to] the Maria Duval story."

He said this did not mean he didn't want to meet us, however, saying he might call us and invite us out for a drink next time he was in town. He ended by wishing us both a Merry Christmas and "all the best."

Wait, so he didn't actually want to meet with us abroad, like Patric had told us? Why on earth would this Patric guy try to convince us to go all the way to Thailand? And if Jean-Claude really didn't know him, who was he? We too had heard of a man named Patrice; in fact, this was the same man our "Secret Friend" had called crazy and unpredictable. One of the Patricks whom Jean-Claude was referring to was likely the French psychic Patrick Guerin. We needed to email Jean-Claude again, this time to ask if he was positive he didn't know this man, who claimed to be his childhood friend.

"First, my childhood in Switzerland was 50 years ago and I do not remember any Patric ——. I can also say that as long as I can remember, I never talked to anyone named Patric ——," he wrote back defiantly.

Determined to figure out what was going on, we wrote back again, giving more details that Patric had provided to us, including that he claimed to have visited Jean-Claude in Thailand just a few years earlier. To this claim, Jean-Claude legitimately seemed to be just as bewildered as we were. "I have no idea who is this man," he wrote, saying that if he had visited him in Thailand recently, then his name was "definitely NOT" the one he had given us.

We weren't sure what to make of this but were sure of one thing: we weren't going to Thailand.

. . .

It started with the filmmaker, who was convinced that a satanic cult was at the root of the scheme, and that many of the businessmen were involved. Scary enough on its own, this claim also made us think of the frightening theories we'd read online about the secret societies Antoine was involved with. Then came the weird emails from Romania from the "journalist" and the "secretary," reminding us of a game of Clue.

A number of anonymous tipsters had also warned us that there were very wealthy and dangerous people involved in the scheme. "I've helped you enough by now. Need to keep my distances," our "Secret Friend" told us. Then we'd heard from the man claiming his name was Patric, who for some reason was trying to lure us to Thailand to meet with Jean-Claude. But after Jean-Claude told us he had no reason to meet with us, we questioned whether "Patric" might have had other motives. Nothing was out of the question—including our being thrown into the ocean from the beaches of Thailand, never to be seen again. Our minds were racing as we tried to figure out how all of this might be connected, feeling trapped inside a psychological thriller that just wouldn't end.

We returned to where it all started, with the filmmaker. This time he wouldn't return any of our emails or phone calls. The num-

ber we reached him at the first time seemed to be registered to someone else entirely. With our minds already in a dark place, we asked
ourselves if he could be linked to these other people as well. He had
provided us with only his first name, but we thought we'd been able
to deduce his last name from his email address. We searched public
records to try to find any other contact information for him. The
only person with that name was a disturbed young man who had
been charged with killing his father but had recently been acquitted
of murder by reason of insanity.

What had we gotten ourselves into?

The Return to Sanity

WRAPPED UP IN our own paranoia, we tried to convince ourselves that we had nothing to fear. If even half of what we'd been told was true, it was Maria who had every reason to be just as scared as her son said she was.

To date, we hadn't seen a single shred of physical evidence that Maria was actually alive. The last physical trace of her was a signature on court documents from the US government settlement. But even this signature seemed suspicious.

Located within hundreds of pages of court documents, the signature meant she was agreeing that letters using her name and image would never be sent in the United States again. On closer examination, we noticed that both of the forms she'd signed were missing key information. While the settlement agreement filled out by Patrick Guerin included the name and signature of the notary who'd verified that he signed the document, Maria's agreement included nothing but a stamp—supposedly from a notary in Provence, France, but with no name or signature. Even stranger, the printed version of her name underneath the signature was spelled incorrectly—it was missing an "L," so it read "Maria Duva." On a second form, many of the required fields, like phone number and email address, had been left blank. And even if it were Maria who had signed the form, it would have been almost a year ago, so there was no way to know if she was still alive today.

Aside from the signature, the most recent evidence of Maria had come from a year earlier, when she was seen picking up her pot of jelly. So we decided to try getting back in touch with the town hall in Callas to see if anyone had seen her.

The year before, its employees had been willing to help, giving us Maria's home address and telling us about the jelly she'd picked up. This time, the woman who answered the phone seemed hesitant to tell us anything, saying that she had a directory of everyone who came to pick up jelly this holiday season, but that she couldn't tell us whether Maria was on this list.

Once again, Maria's son, Antoine, was our last shot.

Since leaving Callas, we'd tried to reach Antoine numerous times with the hopes of finally speaking with Maria ourselves, even if it was just over the phone. He claimed she was alive and kept promising that at the least he would answer more of our questions and possibly even facilitate an interview. But then he would go dark for weeks.

· · ·

For a while, we wondered if the "filmmaker," the "Romanians," and "Patric" were all the same deranged person, one who had lured us into his or her own twisted game. We started to come back to reality when we finally received a call from the filmmaker. He seemed unfazed by his months of silence, telling us he had a day job and had been very busy. He was also willing to give us his full name, as long as we didn't print it. To our relief, a quick search showed us that the biography he gave us about himself checked out. He was definitely not the young man who killed his father.

Whew.

With his identity confirmed, we thought it far less likely that all the messages we'd recently received were part of some broader conspiracy. Still, we were no closer to figuring out who this so-called Patric character was and why he'd reached out to us.

After Jean-Claude's confusion, Julia got back in touch with Patric. He became extremely defensive, saying snidely that if we were already in touch with Jean-Claude then we apparently didn't need him anymore. For some reason, he continued to want to meet us in person.

Jean-Claude, annoyed with all of our questions about Patric, stopped responding to our emails. However, as we looked through his past messages, we saw that perhaps unwittingly Jean-Claude included his cell phone number. With nothing to lose, we broke down and called him in Thailand.

He answered right away in a very friendly voice and was surprisingly courteous even after we told him who we were. It was surreal to actually be talking with him after all the months of emailing back and forth with the man. We spoke for an hour. When we brought up Patric, he again said he didn't know a man with the full name we had been given. He did have an idea of who it might be, though. He also described a childhood friend of forty years, who he said was the only person he knew with a name that came close to Patric's. According to Jean-Claude, the friend's most recent visit had been around a decade ago, not a mere three years as "Patric" had claimed to us.

Despite Patric's claim, Jean-Claude remained adamant that he was not the mastermind behind the Maria Duval letters. Instead, he told us he simply knew her through acquaintances in the mail-order industry such as Jacques Mailland. Jean-Claude also said that the former friend claiming to be Patric had met Maria only once, twenty years ago, maybe in the resort town of Cannes. "I had a drink with him and Maria," Jean-Claude told us.

Jean-Claude also had some theories as to why this man would be telling us false stories about him. He said that while they had been close for a long time, this man had become jealous of him and that something had happened during his most recent trip to Thailand that put an end to their friendship. "To be honest, the meeting [in Thailand] did not end up very nicely," he said. "The relationship ended up badly. I don't think he has a very positive opinion of me."

Given this man's vengeful motives, Jean-Claude told us that nothing "Patric" said could be trusted and that anything he claimed to know about Maria was also likely suspect, given their single meeting over one drink so many years ago.

The Bizarre Businessman Revisited

J EAN-CLAUDE SPENT MUCH of our hour-long conversation be-
rating us for our portrayal of him in the articles we'd published
months earlier, even comparing us to Maria Duval, in an unexpected
way. "Maria Duval would never do any of this to people; she was very
kind, a very kind person. She would not lie. She would not tell stories
that were not true," he said. "I hope you can look at yourself in the
mirror and be happy and proud, but if I were you I would not be."

He told us it was completely unfair to connect him to Maria's
letters, since he claimed his company was nothing more than a ful-
fillment center for all kinds of businesses, including the Maria letters, comparing the circumstances to how the postal service
facilitates mailings but is not involved with their contents. And it
was true that he had never been ensnared by the various government
actions over the years or charged with any wrongdoing. But for
someone not involved with her letters or her operations, Jean-Claude
had somehow gotten to know Maria pretty well.

While at first he told us that he didn't want to speak with us
about her, saying she was the one best suited to do that, he gradually
began to open up. He told us he'd met her decades earlier, when her
local reputation was building in the South of France and she was

dealing with a company in Monaco—where we'd traveled to in search of the shadowy attorney Andrea Egger.

"She was an entertaining person," he said, saying that they enjoyed wine together over the years and that she was full of great jokes.

He also definitely didn't doubt her powers. "She's been in this for a long time and she has the most amazing testimonials from the police and locals there, they all know her as someone who can help people," he told us. "I met people and they told me stories and I got goose bumps. . . . It's amazing what she can do with her gift. She's not a fake."

When we asked if he'd ever received a personal reading from Maria, he said that she would occasionally send him a written one, but that they were too long and technical for his liking. "I don't know if it was one of the things she sends the others," he said, presumably referencing the letters at the center of our investigation. He said he prefers in-person consultations, and he told us that he'd had a "once in a lifetime" experience with a different psychic in Geneva.

Although he seemed to know a lot about Maria and appeared to have spent a good amount of time with her, he said that Jacques, whom she was in business with for many years, knew her much more closely. "They met before I met both of them," he told us. "I know it was a long story behind it. He always worked with psychics and I always knew they were good friends."

And unlike what Antoine told us about her name becoming a runaway train, Jean-Claude didn't make it sound like anyone had taken advantage of her. "She's not naive in business; she's been in business a long time," he said. Though to hear Jean-Claude tell it, this was a compliment, since he didn't view anything she'd done as a scam.

He said that not only was Jacques a close friend of Maria's, but that he was the brains behind the entire operation. This description

sounded a lot like that of the "mailing genius" we had heard him referred to as before. Jean-Claude also confirmed Jacques's 2015 death,
saying that he'd sent flowers to his family but did not attend the funeral. Given Jacques's integral role in the business, Jean-Claude believed the letters would struggle to survive without him.

The Fading Myth

I N A FEW years, a lot had changed for the Maria Duval letters.

In late 2014, the US government began its strongest efforts to date to shut down the scam for good, temporarily freezing its North American operations and eventually wiping out the US business two years later.

Around the same time as the US government's lawsuit, the Swiss company Infogest, which had long been linked to the letters, appeared to go bankrupt. Then Jacques Mailland, the man who seemingly kept the letters alive for so long, died in a motorbike accident in 2015, leaving the scam's operations in uncertain hands. And perhaps most important of all, the woman at the center of the scheme was becoming increasingly ill.

With all of this taken together, it would make sense that the scam's once widespread reach would be fading. Already we had noticed other traces of the scam beginning to disappear. Maria Duval websites around the world went inactive. Consumer complaints about new letters became rare. The long-standing trademarks for her name were allowed to expire. It seems she hadn't made a media appearance in years.

It was possible that the Maria Duval letters were still going out in far-flung locations abroad—perhaps Romania, where those weird emails had come from. But no longer did it appear to be the massive scam that it once was.

. . .

It was Maria's real psychic fame that had made her such a valuable commodity. And much of what made the scam so successful was the fact that there really was a woman out there named Maria Duval. There had always been a glimmer of reality in the myth, perhaps more than we ever would have thought. So if Maria really was dying, we were starting to suspect the scam could die with her.

As she became sicker and sicker over the years, she was apparently no longer willing or able to be the public face of the scam and defend it to the world. And without the woman herself, the letters were losing their power.

We still couldn't believe it. More and more, Maria reminded us of the sick and elderly people her letters so heartlessly targeted.

Along our journey, we had heard the stories of so many of her victims. On one of the very first days of our reporting, we learned of an eighty-eight-year-old US military veteran who'd sent Maria at least eighty-eight checks, each for $45 (adding up to nearly $4,000), in the hope of winning the lottery so he could afford a room in an assisted-living facility.

In the months and years that followed, we continued to hear more of these stories. For one Charlotte, North Carolina, man, the name Maria Duval brought back memories of the months he spent trying to tear his then 101-year-old aunt from the psychic's grasp. He told us he was shocked to discover she had sent Maria $6,000 in a single year. From across the globe in Belgium, a story reached us of an elderly man and his wife, who would walk to the post office multiple times a day to mail check after check to Maria. They stayed awake at night, carefully reading their mail to ensure that they had followed all the requirements and deadlines. "My father passed away three years ago," his daughter wrote to us, "his last few years made more difficult by his manic depression and his obsession about his receiving a large sum of money, thanks to Maria Duval."

The Irony

M ORE THAN ANY other victim, Doreen and her tragic story
continued to return to us as we investigated Maria.

As we sat across from Chrissie at her winter home in Arizona,
hearing about her mother's early days, the woman she described was
nothing like the gullible victim she eventually became. Doreen would
have been horrified to see her future self throwing away the money
she had worked so hard to save.

As with Doreen, behind so many victims was a former self who
would have known better. In Doreen's case, she was always a frugal
woman. At a time when many women were relegated to the kitchen,
Doreen proudly took control of her family's finances. She ensured all
bills were paid on time. She made smart investments for her and her
husband Eric's golden years. She spent most of her life working, starting on factory assembly lines at the age of sixteen, before later manning the cash register at local department stores, founding her own
small business, and managing a local tax-preparation firm.

Born in Edmonton, England, an industrial town on the outskirts
of London, in November 1930, Doreen entered the world a smiling
baby with bright blond curls. Soon everything seemed to crash down
around her as World War II and the bombings that came with it

raged on across the United Kingdom, forcing her family to send her away to the safety of a relative's house as a young girl.

Three years after the war ended, her life having returned to some sense of normalcy, she met her husband while working at an electric cable manufacturer. He was an apprentice to an electrical engineer and was in her building for a job he was tasked with. Doreen was eighteen; he was nineteen. She was short with light blue eyes, he was tall with dark brown ones. She was a social butterfly and loved attending party after party. He preferred being outside camping and hiking, or playing cribbage at home. They married a few years after meeting.

Chrissie describes her mother as social, strong, and controlling. When we asked her if Doreen was adventurous, she laughed at the thought, before remembering one giant risk her mother did take: in 1965, with four young children and two corgis in tow, Doreen and Eric picked up their life and moved four thousand miles away to a country they had never even visited. At the time, England was still rebuilding from the war, and both Doreen and Eric were struggling to get ahead. They were immediately drawn to the idea of starting a new life in a country with a strong economy after watching a documentary-style film that had advertised the promise of Canada.

They shuffled all their kids into a taxi, and then onto a train. From there, they promptly boarded a large ship destined for Toronto. They would spend two long weeks before coming up the Saint Lawrence River. Once in Toronto, they boarded a plane to their final destination of Edmonton, Alberta—which just happened to have the same name as Doreen's hometown in England.

In Canada, they moved into a new suburban development with rows of cookie-cutter homes. Theirs was a four-bedroom stucco bungalow with a large, grassy backyard, a luxury compared with what they'd been used to in England. They lived a solidly middle-class life there, giving their children new clothes for school and taking regular road trips in their family's Ford Meteor.

It was in Canada that Doreen and Eric realized their dream of launching their own business, a small store called Robinson's Pet and Hobby. Housed in a local shopping mall, the store became a hodge-podge of art supplies and small animals. Guinea pigs, fish, hamsters, and birds shared space with knitting tools, paint, and other crafts. Doreen taught the occasional art class and groomed dogs in the back room, and Eric held diorama-making competitions for local school-children. Their kids were expected to help out around the store as well, cleaning pet cages or following around any mischievous-looking children who Doreen worried might take off with a piece of merchandise. They were paid not in money but in items pulled straight from the store's shelves.

In both her work and her personal life, Doreen was undyingly sensible, sometimes to a fault. Childhood accidents prompted a careful Band-Aid, but little sympathy. Her children received their first bikes as gifts, but when they outgrew them they were expected to earn their own money to buy new ones. When they threatened to run away, she would offer to help them pack their bags. She didn't believe in saying "I love you." Decades later, her grandchildren were equally fearful of receiving one of their grandma's "famous disciplinary looks."

Her family members knew that all this came from a place of love and that she cared deeply for them. Chrissie remembers the time she fell on a piece of glass, slashing her wrist wide open, and how her mother promptly but calmly used the first aid skills she'd learned during her teenage years in the Sea Rangers, a British sailing and rowing organization for young women, clamping Chrissie's wrist tightly and shoving her into the car. "With instructions to hold my hand high as she packed me in the car, I witnessed my mother speeding for the first time in my life, honking the car horn madly at every intersection on our way to the hospital," Chrissie told us. "Through any of our emergencies, our mother never hesitated, broke down in tears, or became faint."

And there were times when another, softer side of Doreen came out.

All four kids would look forward to nights curled up on the couch, when Doreen would let them take turns cuddling up behind her knees and by her side. She loved to spoil herself with drugstore romance and mystery novels for her ever-expanding book collection and new supplies for all her artistic endeavors. She was endlessly creative, winning awards for her intricate needlepoints that she would spend months to make, painting nature scenes on canvas of all sizes, and crocheting everything from blankets to baby clothes anytime she heard of a friend or family member welcoming a new baby.

The fashionable Doreen bought more clothes than she could ever possibly wear, not going out in public without looking perfect. "When I was very small, I remember watching her apply lipstick before going shopping, amazed she could color in the lines of her lips without even glancing in the mirror right beside her," Chrissie recalls.

Her sister-in-law remembers how Doreen would insist on walking through the forest with her husband while wearing "the highest of high heels." "How she never broke her ankle I just can't imagine, although I imagine Eric was holding her pretty tightly!" she later told family and friends at Doreen's funeral.

Throughout their nearly fifty years together, Eric never stopped worshipping Doreen. When Eric was diagnosed with colon cancer, Doreen was his caretaker until the very end.

He died just after the turn of the century. To keep busy, Doreen quickly booked her days full of social activities, staying active in her church, going on shopping trips, and meeting friends for tea and gossip. Soon after she sold the bungalow where she and Eric had lived for all those years, she moved into a new condo. Despite her insistence that she was fine on her own and even enjoyed her newfound independence, Doreen insisted on holding on to Eric's ashes and wanted her own to be combined with his when her time eventually came. She seemed happy most days and would never admit to her children that she was lonely, but there were times when she would invent excuses for them to visit her, like needing help hanging a shelf or tending her gardening.

In the days after Doreen died, her son was going through the many boxes filled with her belongings and was amazed to find a poem that she had shared with his father in the early days of their courtship. At Doreen's funeral he read the poem aloud as his voice cracked and faltered. It was a beautiful reminder of their parents' love, the perfect way to remember their mother.

Here was Doreen, twenty years old at the time, speaking to them, all these years later, as her ashes were combined with her husband's in a small hole dug in the grass, and the cold breath of her friends and family circled up into the bright afternoon sky.

I do believe that God above created you for me to love.
And picked you out from all the rest because He knew
    I'd love you best.
I once had a heart called mine 'tis true, but now it's
    gone from me to you.
Take care of it as I have done, for you have two and I
    have none.

If I go to Heaven and you're not there, I'll paint your
face on a golden star
So all the angels can know and see just what you really
mean to me.
If you've not come by Judgement Day, I'll know you've
gone the other way
So I'll give the angels back their wings, the golden harp
and everything
And just to show you what I'll do, I'll go to Hell dear,
just for you.
Love, Doreen, August 17, 1950

. . .

When it became clear that Doreen's mind was failing her, she was one of the first to admit that she should no longer be living on her own.

She entered an assisted-living facility in the fall of 2010, where she was happy. She showed off her flexibility in yoga classes and made funny faces in photos in which she donned silly, homemade hats. She drank wine and shared stories with new friends. She danced at parties and sang in a painfully off-key voice, declaring to anyone who protested, "So what, I'm enjoying myself . . . pooh to you!"

There she was free from Maria. But soon enough, other demons took their hold. "A bit like an old black & white TV with damaged rabbit ear antennas," Chrissie wrote in an email to her brothers in the summer of 2011. "She goes in and out & some days are better than others & you have to hold the rabbit ears a certain way and not move at all, even then the picture does the intermittent vertical spin. Lately the TV barely flickers on."

As more than a year passed since she first moved into the new facility, there were clear signs that the Doreen her family knew and loved wasn't coming back. When one of her sons took her to get a new ID card, and Doreen was asked to sign the necessary form, she wrote the word "Signature." After buying balls of blue yarn and a pattern to knit a baby blanket for her forthcoming great-grandson, she defiantly stated that the pattern was too confusing and that the directions weren't written in English (which they were). And after repeated bursts of crying, from a woman who rarely cried, and even threats to jump off the roof, she ended up spending much of her time locked in the facility's "memory lane" ward, where the more severe dementia patients were relegated.

Then a horrible accident in which Doreen fractured her pelvis after being pushed to the floor by another resident forced her to leave the community she once loved. She moved to a facility that provided full-time care, a nursing home in Edmonton, Alberta, that Chrissie remembered reeking of death. It was here that the realization that Doreen had lost all control of her mind, her body, and even her own decisions dawned on her family. Her children say this is where Doreen's transformation into a different person was completed.

It started innocently enough. "One time, she wasn't happy with what the doctor said and stomped off in the opposite direction, giving an angry glance over her shoulder toward the doctor," Chrissie recalled during her eulogy. "The only thing missing was her sticking out her tongue."

But soon after, when she came down with the flu and was bed-ridden for a week, she forgot how to walk. Then came the frightening phone calls Chrissie received from the nursing home, when Doreen became increasingly aggressive toward the staff and the other residents. One day she either tried to, or actually did, hit a man with her walker. Another day, she attempted to strangle her roommate. When Chrissie tried to speak with her over the phone, Doreen pretended to be fast asleep.

Her family was worried about what else would happen to her there. Chrissie had to do something. So she moved her eighty-two-year-old mother into yet another nursing home, the third unfamiliar place she had entered in a mere three years. Here, at least, Doreen experienced small "moments of respite from the horrors that only she could see."

• • •

Something had taken hold of Chrissie.

For the life of her, Chrissie can't remember what made her do this. It was the only time in her nearly sixty years of life that she'd resorted to ranting online, four years after she discovered her mom's tragic obsession. Hunched over her laptop after a long day with her mother at the nursing home, she says she lost control of her fingers as she angrily pounded the keyboard.

> My mother, a smart, educated, in-charge woman who was a lonely widow living in the small town of St Albert, Alberta, Canada, surviving on a small pension, fell for this scam! Unfortunately, my mother was also exhibiting early signs of Alzheimer's. She didn't realize that sending $59 every week was adding up. She didn't understand the silly amulets she sometimes received in a lovely velveteen bag were nothing but a two cent piece of junk! I've read other rip-off reports about this place and it still angers me 4 years later how this company has manipulated people's emotions to make money hand over fist.
>
> . . .
>
> Did it bring my mother luck? health? wealth? happiness? No, No, No, No!

Doreen died two days later.

. . .

It feels surreal to us how this story unfolded from that first psychic letter we pulled from a pile of junk mail. Even the characters we discovered along the way could easily be culled from a mystery novel. The gun-toting postal investigators who dug through Dumpsters. The curious accountant holed up in a nondescript office space in Shakespeare's birthplace. The Swiss businessman who was part of an alien-worshipping religion. The mailing genius who supposedly met his untimely demise in a Parisian motorcycle accident. The harrowing French drive that almost killed us too. The mysterious man with all the mailboxes. The shady attorney with the Monaco high-rise. The male crime reporter who somehow ended up writing fantastical letters in the voice of a female psychic. The dancing Hawaiian sushi chef in the same strip mall where millions of dollars were once sent to Maria. The pot of jelly that brought Maria out of hiding. The filmmaker convinced that this was all part of a broader global satanic conspiracy. The self-proclaimed secretary for the psychic, based in Romania. The supposed childhood friend who tried to lure us to the beaches of Thailand. The missing people miraculously found.

As we filed away our notebooks once and for all, we knew where the letters had originated so long ago, and with Maria on—or near—her deathbed, we were pretty sure the infamous Maria Duval scam was finally coming to an end. There was one big question that remained. Even after our incredible journey and all the discoveries that we'd made along the way, we wondered: Did Maria understand the sheer magnitude of the scheme, a heartless and practically unstoppable con that couldn't have existed without her? We still weren't sure she fully grasped her pivotal role in all of this.

We remain struck by the twisted irony of it all. In the two years that Maria Duval consumed our lives, she transformed from a beautiful, glowing young woman to a weak, frightened old lady.

Just like her victims. Just like Doreen.

Both Maria and Doreen had started out working hard to earn their money, running their own small businesses. They were strong, independent women who deeply valued their appearance. And their final years were marked by a painful decline.

We were left to wonder if Maria, who was now holed away in her gated house, afraid to show her face to the world, would perhaps have done this all differently. Did she have any last regrets or see herself as a defiant martyr proud of all the good she believed she had done? Was she remorseful, ashamed of the pain she had caused so many?

Surely she would have changed course long ago if she had known that this was how it would all end, with her name now synonymous with fraud and greed rather than the selfless benevolence she long proclaimed, with countless businessmen raking in far more money than she could ever imagine, with millions of lives destroyed in her wake. We would like to believe that she never would have signed that first fateful contract, the arrangement her son described as a deal with the devil.

If Maria really was a psychic, wouldn't she have seen this all coming?

Afterword

I T SOUNDED LIKE something out of a movie. The publication of our book was rapidly approaching when we heard from Maria Duval's son that something shocking had happened. The US government had sent an investigator and two attorneys all the way to Maria's tiny town in the south of France.

French police joined the same USPIS investigator who first discovered this scam, at the same gate that we became so familiar with two years earlier. As Antoine described the scene, police entered Maria's home with a money-sniffing dog that roamed her large property and garden. The police opened drawers, seized her computer, took piles of documents, and pulled bank account records for both Maria and her family. US officials had once written that they didn't even know if Maria was a real person. Now the key investigator was at her house. Antoine claimed the raid was all about recovering proceeds from the scam, but he said they didn't find a cent. During an hours-long Skype conversation, he insisted that his mother had only a few thousand euros left in her dwindling accounts. He also finally revealed the extent of her sickness, saying that she had been battling the effects of Alzheimer's disease for several years.

With this mission to France, the US government had been hoping to get answers from Maria. Instead, according to Antoine, Maria couldn't remember her name when asked by police, and was deemed incompetent by investigators based on a physician's assessment of her condition. She was therefore unable to sit for an interview. So Antoine went instead, sitting in a room in the local police station for six hours talking to the postal inspector, two attorneys from the Department of Justice, and French police who officially conducted the interview.

They asked him a lot about the money his mother made. They were also very interested in the businessmen. Antoine said three names kept popping up: Jean-Claude Reuille, the retiree holed away in Thailand; Lucio Parrella, the Swiss man who had been one of the most recent contacts we could find for the scam but claimed his only involvement was to help sell her books; and Andrea Egger, the mysterious attorney in Monaco. Up until this point, we had never heard the US government mention these names. Their public filings to date had focused on lower rungs of the scheme, and we hadn't been sure whether any investigation was ongoing after the scam had been shut down in the United States. If what Antoine was telling us was true, it meant that the US government was finally investigating the people we believed were central to this scam. Antoine said that when asked if he would be willing to testify in any legal proceeding that may take place in the United States, he said yes.

At the end of our conversation, Antoine told us something else. Perhaps because of how angry he was about the government's focus on his mother instead of the businessmen, he said he would finally let us see Maria. At first he offered to set up a Skype call where we could simply wave hello and goodbye, but when we asked if we could return to France to meet her in person instead, he agreed.

Three weeks later, we boarded a plane in a daze. We landed at the same airport in Nice, this time careful to take the toll roads as we drove to the same hotel. As the hours to our meeting ticked down, we still wouldn't let ourselves believe that this was actually going to happen. It was a Saturday in early May when we rang the same doorbell we had cursed so many times before. Once the gate opened, we drove down the long, narrow driveway and took in our first glimpse of Maria's home, which was surrounded by overgrown grass littered with statues of naked Greek gods, monkeys, and elephants. We had made it to the other side.

The day unfolded almost like dream. The night before, we had made a list of all the ways this meeting could go horribly wrong—even ending in our untimely demise. Instead, Antoine, his wife, and two of his daughters greeted us with smiles and led us toward Maria's house. At the top of the stairs stood Maria, the woman who had been our sole obsession for years. She wore blue Crocs, cartoon-covered socks, faded leopard-print leggings, a chunky black sweater, and a red necklace. She looked at us with a blank stare as we took turns shaking her hand.

It was clearly the same woman, but she was a shell of herself. Her eyes were confused; her large lips looked almost deflated; her lipstick was drawn outside the lines; and the defensive, confident woman we had seen in the past was nowhere to be found.

We followed her and Antoine farther into the house, starting in her personal office, a small room filled with shelves upon shelves of vinyl three-ring binders, paintings of wizards and crystals, photos of herself, and endless trinkets that appeared to be from all around the world. From there, a hallway filled with even more binders led us into the room we had been waiting for. Antoine described it as the office where she did her consultations, and we immediately recognized it from the YouTube videos, with the Virgin Mary statues, crystal ball, and large wooden desk. While we weren't able to tour her entire house, the rooms we did see were in disrepair and seemed to be relics from a past life of fame and fortune. As we flipped through stacks of binders full of newspaper and magazine clippings, her face was everywhere. In horoscope columns, on the pages of French *Vogue*, on clippings about

TV and radio shows throughout the 1970s and 1980s. We knew she had been a well-known local psychic but hadn't ever realized the extent of her fame. Antoine told us that his mother had been paid so well for these media appearances and writings that she had been a very wealthy woman before ever getting involved with the businessmen. He said that everything, including the money, went downhill after she sold her name. We had been skeptical that a psychic could become such a highly paid celebrity, but now it seemed plausible. Maria watched us look through all of these articles without saying anything.

We had been dreaming of this meeting for years and had a list of tough questions we were determined to ask her, hoping Antoine was exaggerating his mother's condition as a convenient excuse to avoid US authorities. But as we sat across from her in her office, she was happy to be on camera but was unable to even tell us the day or answer basic questions about her life and psychic abilities—repeating herself and struggling to find or complete words. It was clear that the woman with the answers to all of our questions was gone.

She soon left to go upstairs to rest, and we sat with Antoine and his daughter Solène to ask them the questions we couldn't ask Maria. But her family only knew so much, and still claimed to be unaware of the full extent of Maria's business dealings, saying they wished they had known what she had gotten herself into sooner so that they could have found out more. Antoine again told us he didn't know how much money she had ultimately made from selling her name and claimed that the royalties had stopped coming. He remained adamant that she had received only a fraction of what others had. Antoine would of course have an incentive to tell investigators, and us, there was nothing to find. But if she was truly penniless, how was she still living in such a large and expensive house that would surely require pricey upkeep? Antoine said she had purchased the house before getting involved with the letters, and that he and his family had been paying the bills.

Then we asked a question we had long wondered about: whether his mother was really in Rome the last time we had come to speak with her, two years ago. He and his daughter looked at each other uncomfortably and laughed. The voice from the other side of the gate who told us Maria was in Rome had not been that of a housekeeper. The voice was Maria's. She had been the woman behind the gate all along, and she had created the elaborate lie to avoid us.

If Maria truly hadn't had anything to hide, why wouldn't she have talked to us? In her right mind, she wanted nothing to do with us. Now she wandered about her property like a lost child, continuing to come into the room to look at us and shake our hands throughout our visit. The Maria sitting before us had become a scammer's perfect target, a perfect victim to place on all those suckers lists that the scam in her own name had relied on.

To hear Antoine tell it, Maria had been like her victims long before she suffered from the debilitating effects of old age. And he acknowledged she was never completely innocent. She had fallen hook, line, and sinker for the unbelievable promises of wealth and fame that were made to her by Swiss businessmen. Businessmen who dazzled her with their expensive suits, luxury watches, and pricey cars, which Antoine believes convinced her to sign on the dotted line without fully understanding the contract she was signing or what she was giving away.

She had been drawn to anything that shines, and she had put her trust in dangerous places.

We placed our laptop on the desk in front of Antoine and played an audio recording of Chrissie, who spoke straight to Maria and blamed her for preying on her mother, a confused, lonely, elderly woman. In that moment, even Antoine couldn't deny the pain his mother had caused by making that deal with the devil—whether she intended to or not.

We had been given the opportunity to sit right in front of this woman, to stare into her vacant eyes. Every dead end, every twist and turn in our journey had taught us so much about Maria and this scam and had finally brought us here. But unlike the movies, we didn't get to choose our ending. We now knew that the woman on the letters would never be able to share her story with the world. And even if we had heard her side, it would have been just that: her story, her claims, all colored by her own perception. It would have done nothing more than satisfy our own curiosity. Say Maria felt some level of remorse or wished she could have gotten out of those contracts she had signed so long ago. None of that mattered now. She couldn't turn back time. No one can ever recover the hundreds of millions of dollars that have been taken from so many victims. Or the billions of dollars taken from so many others by all kinds of mail frauds. Sure, our obsession had started with Maria, but we always knew that this scam was part of a much bigger story.

Across the country, and the globe, we encountered a huge number of individuals willing to prey on the elderly. In many ways, the Maria Duval scam was a perfect case study. It revealed just how many different layers could make up a single fraud, how profitable this kind of scheme could be, how the businesspeople justify their actions, and how victims are so strategically and mercilessly targeted. More than anything else, it showed how a scam could become practically unstoppable. Maria's letters may be coming to an end. But there are countless similar scams that are still going strong and many others just beginning. Each has its own story. Its own cast of characters. None, however, have Maria, the smiling woman in the photo who made one of the longest-running scams in history all possible.

This will always be her legacy.

Acknowledgments

OUR INFATUATION WITH the Maria Duval letters started two years ago, with our multipart investigation for CNN. It's rare that a news organization allows its reporters to embark on this kind of project, and we have many people to thank for their trust in us from the very beginning—no matter how crazy it sounded.

Executive editor Lex Haris didn't flinch when we said we thought we needed to go to France to see this story through, and he was one of the main reasons the two of us became the reporting team we are today, giving us the freedom to pursue out-of-the box but important stories like this one. Our editor, Nicole Ridgway, also believed in the story from the beginning and turned our dispatches into a compelling, chapter-by-chapter series that hooked readers and kept them coming back each week.

Julia Jones, our fearless translator and interpreter, joined this investigation before we headed to France and never let the story go. She made every interview happen and asked the hard questions in a way that always got answers. She became so much more than a translator. She has been a third member of our reporting team and one that was absolutely crucial to this entire journey.

Our literary agent, Eileen Cope, approached us soon after our investigation was published on CNN, telling us we should write a book. Even though we had no idea what this would entail, she somehow managed to land us a deal with one of the best publishers in the country, Simon & Schuster's Atria. She also found us the perfect editor there, Todd Hunter. When we envisioned working with a book editor, we worried about endless revisions and rewrites until the manuscript lost every ounce of our own voice and vision. But this was absolutely not the case with Todd. He understood our vision for this story and every edit he made was intentional, thoughtful, and necessary.

Since writing a book would have been a pipe dream if we hadn't already published this investigation on CNN, we also want to thank everyone who made the original series possible. CNN's superstar attorney Johnita Due, who probably read every word of our series dozens of times by the time it was published and who was more excited about every new twist and turn of our adventure than you would ever imagine a lawyer being. Thank you to Ed O'Keefe and Meredith Artley, who both gave this crazy idea so much support from the beginning. And everyone else at CNN who dedicated so many hours to this project: Jordan Malter and Mark Esplin, who joined us in France and captured many of the incredible moments and scenes from our book on camera so that we will have them forever. Antoine Crouin, another fantastic translator who made our meeting with Maria possible. Contessa Gayles and Lou Foglia, who turned our insane *Homeland* crime board into a creative video to accompany the series. Tiffany Baker, who designed this first-of-its-kind investigation for CNN, and Megan Pendergrass, who brought the wild characters to life through her illustrations. Richard Griffiths and Steve Holmes were also crucial to making sure every word of our series met CNN's ethical and factual standards. And Jan Winburn, who taught us so much about the importance of writing and storytelling in any investigation.

We also spent hours talking to sources who gave us their time and trust. Chrissie Stevens was willing to recount one of the most painful times of her life in telling us about her mother's decline. She welcomed us into her home and went through her memories in such detail that we tried to channel her powerful words in each chapter where we told her story. The whole investigation began because a box of junk mail was sent to us by two women whose relatives had been taken in by scams. It is sources like these women, who are concerned enough about something to make the effort to reach out to a reporter, that make our job so worthwhile. We met a number of other investigators who were just as committed to getting to the bottom of this. Clayton Gerber, a USPIS agent, convinced us that the Maria Duval letters were something more than just a typical mail scam. Journalists, including Jan Vanlangendonck from Belgium and Willem Bosma from the Netherlands, provided us with sources, documents, and information from their own reporting on this scam. Dr. Peter Lichtenberg helped us understand the psychological state of many of the victims who fall prey to scams like this.

Countless readers shared their own experiences with loved ones taken advantage of by this scam, while others emailed us fascinating theories, tips, and new leads along the way.

Finally, a big thank-you to Jim Steele, our investigative reporting and book-writing mentor who has a thoughtful, intelligent answer for every question that comes his way.

Blake

Growing up, I watched my grandfather John Thomas write book after book on his typewriter—carefully editing each sentence and getting rid of stray words and typos with his old-fashioned eraser and brush. I remember seeing the final copies show up in the mail, and I couldn't believe that all those words flowing from his head into that typewriter had been converted into such beautiful books. I knew then that I wanted to do this one day. And while modern-day technology made the process easier, I can't help but be reminded of my grandfather, his curiosity, and his love for writing that provided me with such endless inspiration.

For those of you who were part of this bizarre journey, thank you for being so supportive. Charlie, who listened to every new development along the way, who put up with the dreams of frightening international businessmen that woke me at night, the constant frustration I faced with every dead end we hit, and the questions I blurted out of nowhere. My mom, who loved even the roughest drafts of this story. To the rest of my family and friends—Winston Ellis, Chandler Ellis, John Thomas, Mary Koto, Tory Clark, Lynne Grubbs, Clayton Goodgame, Julianne Pepitone, the Donnellys, the Sayres, the McIntyres, Kim Thai, and Robert Dodge—I am so grateful for your support, your thoughtful feedback, and your continued interest in this mystery.

Finally, none of this would have happened without Melanie, my partner in crime through this whole adventure. You know how to tap into my crazy, and your brilliantly organized mind is the only way we get things done. I can't wait for many more investigations and journeys to come.

Melanie

Long before I became a journalist, I always dreamed of being a published author, and there are countless people who have helped make that goal a reality. I have been fortunate to learn from teachers and editors who have helped sharpen both my senses and my writing. No one has been a bigger cheerleader than my Syracuse University professor and lifelong mentor Charlotte Grimes. Grimes, you taught me to show and not tell and that the best stories are often told in fewer words. For this, and for all of your support and tough edits over the years, including edits of some of these very pages, I am so grateful. To all my friends and family who read various drafts of this book—Jessie Assimon, Laura Stampler, Meghan Directo, my mom, and others— thank you so much for taking time out of your busy lives to give us such thoughtful feedback.

And then there's my family, who put up with this bizarre obsession for the better part of two years. Ryan, I am so lucky to be married to someone who is so supportive of my passions. Thank you for never being annoyed when I checked my phone constantly for Maria Duval updates or when I disappeared for days or weeks at a time to continue this adventure. To my parents, Jim and Julia Hicken, who have nurtured my love for reading and writing since my childhood, thank you for always being my biggest fans. To my brother, Scott Hicken, thank you for always pushing me to think outside the box and to get out of my comfort zone. To my brand-new daughter, thank you for napping so I could finish up final edits. In all seriousness, I am so excited to be your mom and can't wait for you to have this book on your very own bookshelf someday!

And finally to my work wife, Blake: I feel so lucky to get to spend each day working with one of my best friends. Your empathy makes our reporting and writing that much better, while your ability to stay calm in even the most stressful situations still astounds me. From our unforgettable trips to France to our wine-fueled writing sessions, working on this project has been one of the most rewarding experiences of my life. I'm so excited to see what we do next.

Notes

Epigraph

Archived version of MariaDuval.com and MariaDuval.net accessed via the Internet Archive.

The Journalists

Patrick Guerin's letter and video DVD received by elderly source; Department of Justice press release from November 2014, titled "Justice Department Files Enforcement Actions to Shut Down 'Psychic' Mail Fraud Schemes"; online consumer complaints; interviews with family members of victims; "Dump all the mystic messages in the bin," *Evening Chronicle*, February 7, 2002; interviews with the US Postal Inspection Service and information from the agency's website.

The Promises

Maria Duval letter filed as evidence in 2014 US government lawsuit.

The Scam

Maria Duval letters filed as evidence and other documents from 2014 US government lawsuit; Maria Duval Letters; public Maria Duval trademark documents; victim loss estimates for United States and Canada from US Postal Inspection Service.

The Victims

Interviews and written recollections of Chrissie Robinson; online consumer complaints; 2011 elder fraud loss estimate from "The MetLife Study of Financial Abuse"; victim letters filed as evidence in 2014 US government lawsuit; interview with Dr. Peter Lichtenberg; "We Predict a Bleak Future for Maria the Sinister Psychic . . . Maria Duval psychic swindler who offers free good luck talisman," *Sunday Mail*

(London, UK), March 23, 1997; "Praise for river rescue bid; Parents thank heroic officer," *The Journal* (Newcastle, UK), December 31, 1998; "Riverdeath Girl in Psychic Rid," *Sunderland Echo* (Sunderland, UK), December 31, 1998; "Dead teenager's psychic fixation," *Evening Chronicle* (Newcastle, UK), July 29, 1999; "Probe into girl's river death," *Evening Chronicle* (Newcastle, UK), December 31, 1998; "Dump all the mystic messages in the bin," *Evening Chronicle* (Newcastle, UK), February 7, 2002; "Riddle of drowning 'spirit girl,'" *The Mirror* (London, UK), January 1, 1999.

The Address

Maria Duval letters filed as evidence and other documents from 2014 US government lawsuit; email from reader.

The Mysterious Psychic

Maria Duval Wikipedia entry, fall 2015; emails and interviews with private investigator Ron Reinhold; Maria Duval letter provided by Reinhold; "We Predict a Bleak Future for Maria the Sinister Psychic . . . Maria Duval psychic swindler who offers free good luck talisman," *Sunday Mail* (London, UK), March 23, 1997; Astrocat online forum; "Fortune teller's key to happiness unveiled as scam," *New Zealand Herald*, December 18, 2001; 2004 press release from Danish Consumer Ombudsman, "ICPEN Europe Fights Commercial Clairvoyants"; 2006 scam alert from Windsor, Ontario, Police Department; emails from Windsor Police Department; email from Western Australia Department of Commerce; motion filed in 2014 US government lawsuit; emails from psychics; French Maria Duval trademark documents; international Maria Duval trademark documents accessed through the World Intellectual Property Organization; emails with trademark attorneys; YouTube video of media appearance in Finland; audio recording of January 2000 Australian Broadcasting Corporation radio interview conducted by Maria Zijlstra; YouTube video of 2007 interview of Maria Duval, aired on Belgian television program *Koppen*; interview with Belgian journalist Jan Vanlangendonck.

The Psychic Sidekick

Maria Duval and Patrick Guerin letters filed as evidence in 2014 US government lawsuit; Patrick Guerin Facebook page; Patrick Guerin business website; Google Street View.

The Sightings

Flickr photos posted by user named "Maria Duval"; press release about Maria Duval's Russia visit (translated into English); *"Draguignan Maria Duval: le retour que personne n'avait prédit,"* *Var-matin*, December 28, 2008; declaration of Thomas Ninan; documents from 2014 US government lawsuit; YouTube videos posted by user gd2use; news articles from Kazakhstan and Russia.

The Dentist's Wife

Maria Duval YouTube videos; archived versions of MariaDuval.com and MariaDuval.net accessed via the Internet Archive.

The Investigators

US Postal Inspection Service official website; declaration from Postal Inspector Thomas Ninan and other documents from 2014 US government lawsuit; Lawrence County Historical Society website; Robert M. Lombardo, *The Black Hand: Terror by Letter in Chicago* (Urbana and Chicago: University of Illinois Press, 2010); Smithsonian's National Postal Museum website; crimeinnyc.org; archived version of Data Marketing Group website accessed via the Internet Archive; Google Street View.

The Business Web

Domain registrations for Maria Duval's websites; Joseph Davitt's business websites and LinkedIn profile; Google Street View; international business filings; interviews with Barney McGettigan, Gerard du Passage, and a former representative for Maria Duval.

The Sparks Connection

2014 US government lawsuit; obituary for Martin Dettling's relative; interview with Martin's family member.

The Whistleblower

Interview with former Astroforce employee.

The "Mailing Genius"

Interview with Belgian journalist Jan Vanlangendonck; interviews with former employees with knowledge of Jacques Mailland and the Maria Duval letters; Facebook and Google+ profiles for Jacques Mailland; direct marketing conference attendance list posted online; interview with Dutch journalist Willem Bosma; email from Jacques Mailland's Brazilian kitesurfing school; email from Jacques Mailland's business colleague.

The Bizarre Businessman

"*Le piège retors des ventes par correspondance,*" *L'Hebdo*, July 14, 1994; official Raelism website; Swiss government business filings; interview with former colleague of Jean-Claude Reuille; 2005 decision from New Zealand Advertising Standards Authority; Astroforce business filings.

The Copywriter

Maria Duval letters filed as evidence and other documents from 2014 US government lawsuit; interview with copywriter.

The Nucleus

Swiss business filings; interview with Lukas Mattle; online Russian complaints and news articles; Russian Maria Duval website.

The Windfall

Interview with Françoise Barre; Maria Duval, *Comment devenir voyant(e): Pratiques et techniques de la voyance* (Paris: Éditions Henri Veyrier, 1985); L'Estagnol business filings.

The Trip

Email from Antoine Palfroy.

The Dusty Archives

Interview with *Nice-Matin* archivist; archived articles; *"Le sabbat d'une gentille sourcière,"* *Nice-Matin*, October 1, 1992.

The Psychic No One Sees

Interviews with local Callas residents and shop owners.

The House

Maria Duval trademark documents; interview with woman at gate of Maria Duval's house.

The Sister

L'Estagnol business filings; interview with Maria Duval's sister, Marie-Françoise Gamba; interview with former Callas mayor Françoise Barre.

The Pot of Jelly

Interview with Maria Duval's gardener; interview with Callas town hall employee.

The Lover

"Draguignan Maria Duval: le retour que personne n'avait prédit," *Var-matin*, December 28, 2008; interview with alleged former manager.

The Son

Trademarks and websites owned by Antoine Palfroy; official Freemason websites; "France: Where Freemasons Are Still Feared," *Bloomberg News*, April 19, 2012, https://www.bloomberg.com/news/articles/2012-04-19/france-where-freemasons-are-still-feared.

The Attorney

Facebook and LinkedIn profiles for Andrea Egger; Maria Duval trademark documents.

The Deal

Interview with Antoine Palfroy (translated from French to English).

The Myth

"*Quelque pas dans l'étrange*," *Nice-matin*, February 7, 1978.

The Responses

Reader emails.

The Other Psychics

Emails, interview, and website of self-proclaimed astropsychologist Dr. Turi; websites and domain registrations for online psychics Laetezia, Alisha, Rinalda, and Martin Zoller; interview with anonymous employee of Anne Chamfort operation.

The Checks

Treasury Department, US Postal Inspection Service, and Department of Justice case documents and announcements.

The Dark and the Strange

Email from filmmaker; interview with German professor and cult expert; "*Quelque pas dans l'étrange*," *Nice-matin*, February 7, 1978; email from Luis Ramos.

The Romanians

Email from man claiming to be Romanian journalist; email from woman claiming to be Maria Duval's secretary in Romania.

The Childhood Friend

Interview with Patric; emails from Jean-Claude Reuille.

The Return to Sanity

US Department of Justice settlement documents; interview with Jean-Claude Reuille.

The Bizarre Businessman Revisited

Interview with Jean-Claude Reuille.

The Fading Myth

Online complaints; documents from 2014 US government lawsuit; emails from CNN readers.

The Irony

Interviews, diary entries, online comment, emails, and personal mementos from Chrissie Stevens.